DEAD

TRUE STORY OF JENNIFER PAN

BY

ALAN R WARREN

Crimes Canada: True Crimes that Shocked the Nation (Book 19)

Complete Series LINK

DEADLY BETRAYAL

TRUE STORY OF JENNIFER PAN

BY

ALAN R WARREN

ISBN 13: 978-1983547379

ISBN 10: 1983547379

Crimes Canada: True Crimes that Shocked the Nation (Book 19)

Complete Series LINK

ACKNOWLEDGEMENT

Thank you to my editor, proof-readers, and to the cover artist for your support! Also, I must thank my family at home as well as my family on the radio, you take me up!

Aeternum Designs (Book Cover)

It is with great thanks to the publisher, Dr. RJ Parker and Dr. Peter Vronsky for allowing me this opportunity to write this book. I also want to thank the editor, proofreaders and all support staff in helping me with this project.

Crimes Canada Collection

**(Click on Image will take you to Amazon US
These books are available WORLDWIDE on Amazon)**

The Killer Handyman
WILLIAM PATRICK FYFE

C.L. SWINNEY
CRIMES CANADA
TRUE CRIMES THAT SHOCKED THE NATION **VOL. 7**

Hell's Angels
BIKER WARS
The Rock Machine Massacres

RJ PARKER
CRIMES CANADA
TRUE CRIMES THAT SHOCKED THE NATION **VOL. 8**

THE DARK STRANGLER
EARLE LEONARD NELSON

MICHAEL NEWTON
CRIMES CANADA
TRUE CRIMES THAT SHOCKED THE NATION **VOL. 9**

ALCOHOL MURDERS
TRUE STORY OF SERIAL KILLER
GILBERT PAUL JORDAN

HARRIET FOX
CRIMES CANADA
TRUE CRIMES THAT SHOCKED THE NATION **VOL. 10**

PETER WOODCOCK
CANADA'S YOUNGEST SERIAL KILLER

MARK BOURRIE
CRIMES CANADA
TRUE CRIMES THAT SHOCKED THE NATION **VOL. 11**

CLIFFORD OLSON

THE BEAST OF BRITISH COLUMBIA

ELIZABETH BRODERICK
CRIMES CANADA
TRUE CRIMES THAT SHOCKED THE NATION **VOL. 12**

TAKING TORI
THE TRUE STORY OF
TERRI-LYNNE McCLINTIC &
MICHAEL RAFFERTY

KELLY BANASKI
CRIMES CANADA
TRUE CRIMES THAT SHOCKED THE NATION **VOL. 13**

BANDITS & RENEGADES
HISTORICAL TRUE CRIME STORIES

SPECIAL EDITION

EDWARD BUTTS
CRIMES CANADA
TRUE CRIMES THAT SHOCKED THE NATION **VOL. 14**

INVISIBLE VICTIMS
MISSING AND MURDERED INDIGENOUS WOMEN

KATHERINE McCARTHY
CRIMES CANADA
TRUE CRIMES THAT SHOCKED THE NATION **VOL. 15**

COPYRIGHTS

AUDIOBOOKS at RJ Parker Publishing

http://bit.ty/ASTORE-CRIMESCANADA

Our Collection of **CRIMES CANADA** books on Amazon.

http://bit.ly/ASTORE-CRIMESCANADA

TRUE CRIME Books by RJ Parker Publishing on Amazon.

http://ripp.ca/ASTORE-TRUECRIME

ACTION/FICTION Books by Bernard DeLeo on Amazon.

http://bit.ly/ACTION-FICTION

PREFACE

A family of three tied up, each with a gun to their head, "Where's the money? Where's the fucking money?" one of the intruders yelled. A petrified daughter tortured and forced to listen to her parents being shot in cold blood. "I heard shots, like pops," she told the 911 operator, "somebody's broke into our home, please, I need help!" Was this a home invasion? Or something else, more sinister, a deadly betrayal.

The real-life horror story that happened inside the Pan family home shocked their normally peaceful upscale Toronto neighborhood. The Pans were an example of an immigrant family. Hann and his wife, Bich Pan, fled from Vietnam to Canada after the U.S.-Vietnamese war to find a better life. Their daughter, Jennifer, was an Olympic-caliber figure skater, an award-winning pianist, and a straight A student.

The Pans worked their way up in this rags-to-riches story, now living in a beautiful home with luxury cars in the driveway. Was it these expensive items that lured three intruders with guns into their home on the night of November 8, 2010?

Find out what really happened when seasoned true crime reporter and author, Alan R. Warren, takes you through the details as they unfold in this book of a deadly betrayal.

Contents

INTRODUCTION

Many countries in the world have created social classes based on money, power, and inheritance, but Vietnam, which has been strongly influenced by China, had a different system. It was one that divided up the people by education. If you were not among the royalty of the country, classes were divided up by knowledge which could help a person move up somewhat, whereas the farmers and laborers were at the bottom and would always be there.

When people immigrate from such a culture to the west, it's quite often the biggest change that they must realize. It's not the language, culture or even the prejudices, but the fact that you can move your class of living up from just working. The fabric of Vietnam's society was based on ancient philosophy. There were authoritative relationships among the people. This was always the man to the wife, son and daughter, this is where it was sons preferred over daughters.

So it was when Huei Hann Pan was a refugee on a long trip by boat from Vietnam to Canada in the late nineteen seventies, that he dreamed of being able to live with enough to secure a life for the children that he wanted to have.

While Huei Hann Pan watched several others die on the same journey that he was on, he kept focused on being alive and well enough to make it to the new land with all its promises and wealth. He was an honorable man with the deep convictions of dignity, so it was with this heroic effort that he decided that his family would have more.

When Huei Hann Pan was working alongside his wife in an auto factory, he would fill the aimless times with visions of his daughter becoming a doctor, and his son being a mechanical engineer. These were careers that would not only reflect on his children, but on him as a father. Success would be expected from the Pan family.

Many of the first-generation immigrants from Asian countries would see praise as an inhibitor because, once you complimented them, they might feel as though they didn't need to go further or accomplish more. There was always room for improvement and there was no accepting mediocrity.

The children would always be disciplined, respectful and obedient. Huei would show great disappointment in anything that was done poorly by his children. He would require his children to be hard working and, even if they had accomplished something good, praise would not be shown; it was by not getting discipline that they knew they did well.

In the Pan family, the father never felt the need to tell the children that he loved them; it was shown by the way he sacrificed for them every day by working so hard and providing a solid foundation for them to learn from.

This type of parenting is quite often called "Tiger Parenting." This type of parenting quite often requires a tough-love approach which would include very high expectations and inducing guilt as a punishment. It can even go as far as making the child feel as if they wouldn't be loved if they didn't follow their parents' wishes. In fact, those that fail to meet the parents' expectations will be called names, and the parents will take away the children's toys. If the child was doing poorly, the family would not celebrate their birthday or even Christmas holidays.

Quite often tiger parenting would also include restricting the children from activities such as watching TV, playing games, or being part of other children's play dates or sleepovers. The parents would be the ones to choose the activities that the children would be involved in. The primary focus would be the education, school grades could not be below an A, and they should be at least two years ahead of their classmates. Children would only be permitted to be involved in activities that they could be awarded for or win medals.

It was also part of the Chinese culture that the children have a life of duty, respect and to care for their parents and elderly family members. This is in return for their parents sacrificing so much for their children.

Is this the kind of parenting that leads to murder? When the parents raise children to be productive and disciplined members of a society, does it also plant the seed to want to be free from such standards that it will lead the children to kill their own parents?

These are the questions that we are left to ask after such a case that happened in real life in such a relatively peaceful country as Canada.

CHAPTER ONE – FROM RAGS TO RICHES

"Coming together is a beginning, keeping together is a process, working together is success." – Henry Ford

Huei Hann Pan and wife Bich-Ha Pan

Huei Hann Pan was born and educated in Vietnam during the war with the United States. In the late part of the 1970s, Huei Hann Pan attended college in Saigon for four years for tool and die and diesel mechanics. After the war, Vietnam was still in a turmoil. Up to 300,000 South Vietnamese were sent to reeducation camps where many endured torture, starvation and disease. Another 200,000 to 400,000 Vietnamese died at sea in boats trying to escape.

There were an estimated one million refugees from Vietnam that immigrated to the United States, and over 500,000 that moved to Canada, Australia and France. The trip from Vietnam to the shores of Canada was a long one, with many people dying on the boat from disease and starvation. Hann Pan was 26 when he arrived at Canada in 1979, where he settled in Scarborough, which was a suburb of Toronto.

Canada had about 24 million people living in the country at that time; the economy was sluggish with a high unemployment rate. This would be even more of a challenge as Hann never spoke any English or had any money at the time. The influx of refugees had made a significant impact on the country. While most of the Vietnamese refugees settled in Montreal, Hann decided to stay in the Toronto area.

This was where Huei Hann Pan met Bich-Ha Luong, who was also a refugee from Vietnam that relocated to the same area of Toronto. The two had met briefly in Vietnam before but never really got to know each other very well. Bich had immigrated with her father and two siblings. The couple then started to date and fell in love quickly.

The couple were soon married, and both found work in the auto industry for Magna International, an auto manufacturer in Aurora, Ontario. Huei Hann was a tool and die maker, while Bich made car parts. Their salaries were quite poor, so they could only afford a small place in a rougher part of Toronto.

They soon had their two children Jennifer, who was born on June 17, 1986, and Felix born in 1989. They wanted to be able to make a better life for their children than what they left behind in Vietnam. By 2004, they were able to afford a lovely three-bedroom home located at 238 Helen Avenue, Markham, which was an upper middle class neighborhood with very low crime.

It is the role of the first born to be the example for the other siblings, and if the first born is a female, as in Jennifer's case, the burden is even stronger.

Jennifer started to take piano lessons and got involved in youth figure skating competitions. After all, they were both activities for which she could be awarded for a superior performance. These events could also measure Jennifer's unique ability rather than in group sports where it would be the whole team that is judged.

Another activity that Jennifer was a part of was swimming. This was not traditional swimming it was known as "Wushu" which is an ancient Chinese martial art. These activities were chosen for her by her parents. None of these activities were from Jennifer's heart; she was not able to direct her own path into the things that she wanted to do. Anytime that she attempted to try something different, it was said to be wrong, or she was being delinquent.

Jennifer became scared every time she went to a competition for skating or piano. She was petrified of falling on the ice or making a mistake during one of her recitals, as it would be a major disappointment to her father.

Jennifer attended the St. Barnabas Catholic School as her father wanted her raised as a Catholic as he was, not a Buddhist like her mother. She was not allowed to spend time with the other students there as she was to focus on her studies. This made Jennifer feel quite alone as she would never be part of any of the other kids' birthday parties or play dates. She could never have sleepover or parties of her own.

It was in eighth grade that Jennifer felt shunned because she never got the valedictorian at graduation, or any other prizes that she tried for. Jennifer felt a deep sense of shame resulting from what she saw as failure.

Eighth grade is also the time that most teenage girls start to care about their looks and begin to wear make-up, but not Jennifer. Jennifer seldom would wear any make-up or would care about wearing fashionable clothes. Many of the other girls at her school would try to make themselves look sexy by rolling up their skirts and having several of the shirt buttons left open. Meanwhile Jennifer would wear large bulky sweaters and keep her hair in ponytails.

Felix, Jennifer's younger brother by three years, seemed to be less intimidated by their father's drive, and was far less responsive. Felix did have a natural ability to take things apart and rebuild them, as he always wanted to know how things worked. Felix was also a lot closer to his mother, who he felt was comforting, while his father was too controlling.

Felix also seemed to be able to do things that Jennifer never could, like coming home with bad grades from school. In fact, he was doing so poorly in school that they moved him into a private school so he could possibly achieve more. This directed Hann to spend his time trying to direct Felix in a successful direction, as he now felt comfortable with Jennifer with her grades.

Even in his piano lessons, Felix was considered lazy and not nearly as talented as his sister was; and even with the help of Jennifer, he just couldn't accomplish the same level of performance. Felix did not have the same level of pressure on him as Jennifer did from their father, as she was the first born.

Hann still showed no sympathy or support to Felix. In fact, one time when the family was out on a bike ride together, Felix fell and broke his arm. Their father just yelled at him and walked Felix's bike home, leaving him crying on the road alone. In another instance, Hann yelled at Felix for cutting his finger in the kitchen while using a knife, in a way that blamed Felix, asking what they were going to do with him.

Jennifer also played the flute and was part of the school band. She always hung out in the band room, as she felt safe there. Most of the other band students were like Jennifer in her upbringing, and most of them had Asian backgrounds. But Jennifer met what would end up being her closest friends in French class, Topaz Chiu and Adrian Tymkewycz.

It was when Jennifer entered high school that her grades started to go from an A+ to maybe a C or B. In her mind, the universities only decided their acceptance on the student's last two years of marks; therefore, she had plenty of time to make up her grades.

How would Jennifer get around her strict father who paid attention to every detail on her report cards from school? Jennifer would then take that report card and forge it to show all A's by using some white-out and a photocopier.

It would be the test for Jennifer when she brought that first forged report card into her father's den to show him. After she handed her father the report card, he scanned the document for several moments without a word, then he looked up and stared into her eyes.

It was then that Jennifer began to panic and began wondering if he knew, how could he know? It was a long cold stare; did her father know what she was thinking? She could feel the sweat run down her forehead, it was far worse than when she was performing her piano recital or skating in front of crowds for an award.

Hann then smiled slightly and seemed to be his normal self. The faked document worked, and, in fact, he decided that she should work harder on her skating as she had done so well at school. In Jennifer's mind, she could feel the relief as well as the guilt of her first lie that she told her father. She soon rationalized the deceit by thinking that she was getting the same grades as her friends were.

CHAPTER TWO - LOVE WILL SAVE THE DAY

"You can be the moon and still be jealous of the stars" – Gary Allan

Pan Family Home

Another of the behaviors that Jennifer's father had total control of was her personal life. Hann had forbidden Jennifer to date until she was out of university and had an excellent job. Hann had always forbidden her to wear any make-up and never allowed her to cover her acne on her face.

Hann and Bich were not going to let the mistake of a boyfriend ruin the chances of her success; they had spent their lives sacrificing to give their children a bright future. Choosing a husband was a major responsibility that only her parents had the ability to do. In addition, the attention that a relationship would take away from Jennifer at this crucial time in her life was paramount.

Jennifer was romantic and dreamed of the perfect boy over the next two years in high school, not realizing that she was slowly falling for her friend Adrian Tymkewycz. It started innocently from the two of them watching TV together after school or talking on the phone for a long time.

Hann and Bich liked Adrian. He was a good student, very well-mannered and had goals of being an engineer. He had his own car and would be allowed to come to Jennifer's house and visit with the whole family. But as in many young love relationships, it was over within six months, when Jennifer met a new boy.

Jennifer met Daniel Wong in the band room one day, which was the main hang-out for all the music and theatre students. This was where the students would eat their lunch, take breaks or practice their crafts. Unlike the other parts of the school, the music and theatre students tended to be self-motivated rather than directed, which helped create a special bond between the students.

At the start of grade ten, the band department planned a trip to go to Salzburg, Austria, where Mozart was born. Jennifer couldn't wait to go home to tell her parents. This was a big achievement for the band, like an award for all their hard work.

Hann and Bich said no immediately to her request to go, based on a combination of the cost to take such a trip as well as it would be the first time that

Jennifer would be away from home. Jennifer took things into her own hands and began to fundraise by selling chocolates, where she was able to raise $3,000 to put towards the trip.

It would be on this trip that Jennifer found herself noticing Daniel Wong, another band student that she had known, but just never paid any attention to. It was shortly after their first performance in Austria, when they were busing back to their hotel rooms.

Jennifer started to have an asthma attack that caused her to panic. The bus driver pulled over and helped Jennifer off the bus so that she could get some fresh air. The air didn't seem to help her as she fell to the ground and began to pass out. Daniel Wong, the band's trumpet player, came to Jennifer's rescue. He quickly laid her head on his knees and began to coach her into breathing calmly.

It was at this time when Jennifer first felt a love for Daniel. It all seemed so romantic; never had she had a boy show her such attention or display affection to her. This was a whole new experience of emotion that she had never had before. It was only a short amount of time after Jennifer felt rescued by Daniel, that she dropped Adrian and would focus her full attention on Daniel.

Daniel was a far different boy than she had ever really met or hung around with before. He was always laughing and seemed to be having a fun time. Daniel had lots of friends, more than she could have ever imagined; it was so easy for him with his outgoing personality.

Daniel's best friend was black, and they listened to rap and hip-hop music a lot while they would smoke pot. Daniel also loved to play video games and watch movies. This type of lifestyle was all very new for Jennifer.

The two had plenty in common as well, as he was a great piano player like Jennifer was. Daniel had a Chinese father and Filipino mother and cared about being successful as well. It was over their first summer together that she felt she had found her true love.

When they started back at school in the fall, they were forced to spend their time together during school hours, as her father was still picking her up at 3 pm. It was kept a secret from not only Jennifer's parents but most of their friends as well.

Jennifer felt that Daniel loved her unconditionally and would accept her no matter what she decided to do. This was very different for her, as her parents were never interested in her opinion. As Jennifer couldn't phone Daniel from her home, she would write letters to him confessing her love for him, which felt truly liberating for her.

When Daniel turned 18, he moved to a different school that was located on the other side of Toronto, an arts school where he could focus on his music. This made it much harder for him to spend any time with Jennifer, so she decided to start skipping her classes so that she could meet up with him. For the first time, Jennifer had a new priority; it was no longer her schooling, it was Daniel.

Daniel started hanging out at a 24-hour pool hall and bowling alley where he began to sell pot. It wouldn't take long before Daniel started to make good money at his new career, enough to buy a new Audi. Jennifer claimed to have known nothing about Daniel's drug dealing at the time, but later she would admit to delivering pot for him to customers.

As in all activities with risks such as selling drugs, Daniel eventually was caught by the Toronto police. It was one night when he had just bought drugs from his supplier, so when he was pulled over, he had over one pound of pot in his car.

Daniel was soon charged with possession with intent to sell as it was a large enough amount of pot. He pled guilty and gave his source up to the detectives without hesitation, which spared him any prison time. He was also able to keep his parents from finding out about the conviction.

Daniel's trouble didn't end there, as one of his close friends promised to get his Audi detailed for him, but instead was out trying to pick up some women to party with and had an ounce of the horse tranquilizer ketamine in the car. This friend was stopped that night and arrested, which in turn got Daniel a possession charge and his Audi was impounded.

After the second arrest, he decided that he would get away from the bad influences that surrounded him. He stopped going to the pool hall and talking with anybody that he knew from selling drugs. His luxury Audi broke down, and he junked it and bought a Toyota Corolla. He got a job at Boston Pizza as a dishwasher and started attending the York University for music.

At the same time, Jennifer started working at East Side Mario's which was an Italian restaurant at the Markville Mall. This was not to the liking of her father, but he would allow her to work there and use the family car to go to and from work. Hann told Jennifer that the moment any of her studies started to fail, she would have to quit the job.

Jennifer started to take far more risks with her father by starting to tell him lies about activities and work that she was leaving the house to go and do, but she would really go and meet Daniel. Other times, she would even sneak Daniel into the home through her second-story window.

When the couple began to have sex, it became all that they could think about; it became an addiction. But the two were pressed for places to meet, so they would end up having sex in Daniel's car in parks and on dead end streets.

It was 2006 and Facebook became a trendy way for people to communicate with each other. The couple would spend hours texting and chatting on Facebook, even when they were in the bathroom. Jennifer was so focused on planning her every move around seeing or talking with Daniel that she started falling behind in her skating so much that she had to leave the activity.

Jennifer finally would get caught with Daniel one day when her mother saw him dropping her off at the mall. Jennifer was supposed to have been working that day but was really spending the day with Daniel. Bich was waiting at the mall in her car to pick up Jennifer when she finished her shift at work, when she saw Jennifer not only get out of Daniel's car, but hug and kiss him.

This was devastating to Bich, and even though she could sympathize with her daughter, Bich refused to keep it secret from Hann. Jennifer's parents decided that it would be best for them to meet Daniel, so they invited him to a Christmas party at their house.

It seemed that Jennifer's parents didn't like Daniel from the start. Was it the fact that Daniel was half Filipino? In the Asian culture, quite often, the Filipinos were hired as domestic help by other Asians. Was it that Daniel had drug convictions on his record? Daniel and Felix had played video games together and Daniel had told Felix of his drug charges, who in turn told Hann.

There was also the fact that Daniel wasn't making very much money working at Boston Pizza, and he seemed to have no real career goals set for himself. Hann also suspected that Jennifer and Daniel were having sex.

Hann told Jennifer that she was never to see Daniel again. There was never any specific reason given to her from her father. Her mother reassured her that, over time, it would be the best thing for her and things would be good again soon.

This was Jennifer's last year in high school, and she had been accepted into Ryerson University in

Toronto in the science program. This was another disappointment for her father, who had wanted Jennifer to be a doctor and to get into the University of Toronto.

This was the beginning of an even larger deception that Jennifer was about to start, as behind the scenes, Jennifer found out that she was going to fail in calculus and therefore wouldn't receive enough credits to graduate from high school. This would also revoke her acceptance into Ryerson.

It was at this point that Jennifer photoshopped an acceptance letter to Ryerson University with a $3,000 scholarship, as well as graduation photos, and told her parents that she was excited to attend Ryerson University. Her parents were so proud of Jennifer going to university that they had to make sure that she was fully equipped for it. They would spend thousands of dollars getting her a new laptop computer, clothes and even co-signed for a credit card for her. It was important that Jennifer be able to focus on her classes and not have to worry about supplies.

Jennifer staged her plan to the last detail, including going to a library, where she would write several documents filled with information that she obtained from pharmacology websites and books. This would be the perfect cover if her parents or anybody ever checked her work from school.

How long could Jennifer keep this lie going? She would get up every morning and dress, catch the bus to school and spend the day writing out papers in the library. When she came home, she would have to tell her parents about her day.

Jennifer would have to keep notes of the details that she created about her day, so that she wouldn't get the names of professors or classes mixed up. She spent far more time working out the details to tell her parents than she would have just taking the course needed to finish her high school.

CHAPTER THREE - SYMPATHY FOR THE DEVIL

"It's sad when someone you know becomes someone you knew." – Henry Rollins

Lenford Crawford Text to Jennifer Pan on 11/8/10

LC: To after work ok will be game time

After a couple of months of Bich driving Jennifer to university five days a week, Jennifer was able to talk her mother into agreeing to letting Jennifer stay at her friend Topaz's apartment in Toronto from Mondays to Wednesdays, to save the stress of the long travel to school. Bich talked to Hann and convinced him that it would be a good move.

Instead of staying with her friend Topaz for the three days a week, Jennifer was staying with Daniel at his family's home, in the spare room. Jennifer had told Daniel's parents that it was okay with her parents for her to stay with them.

It wasn't long before, instead of three days a week, Jennifer would stay all five days through the week. She would have to call her parents every morning before school so that they would feel comfortable knowing that Jennifer was okay.

Jennifer would also call her parents each night before bed and tell them about her day at school. She would, of course, spend every weekend at home so as not to raise any suspicions. This went on for two years, and she became quite attached to Daniel's parents, who also loved her, as she seemed to be a good influence on their son Daniel.

It was at this point that Jennifer started coming under questions by her father as to what she was going to do next. It was then that she told him that she was transferring to the University of Toronto for pharmacology. Jennifer continued to bring home false report cards to her parents that showed her getting A+, A, or A- on all classes.

Jennifer's graduation was approaching fast, and Hann started asking about how he could buy the tickets to go to her ceremony. Jennifer had to quickly come up with a lie, so she told him that there were so many people attending the graduation that she could only get one ticket. Jennifer didn't want to have to choose between her two parents as to which one should go, so she gave away her one ticket to a classmate.

Later when Jennifer got back home from her supposed graduation ceremony, Hann asked to see the pictures of her accepting her diploma, and she told him that her friend had taken all the pictures and was on a flight to Hong Kong, so she couldn't get them.

Jennifer was able to present him with her degree, which was false; she had bought it off the internet for $500. And it was good enough for him to believe, but not good enough to get a real job with, so she had to create a job now for him to continue to believe in her.

So Jennifer told her father that she was going to be a volunteer at the Toronto Hospital for Sick Children, one of Canada's best-known hospitals for children. Her job was in the blood lab where she would work nights and weekends which would give her enough hours to be given a practical test to prepare her for her career.

Jennifer had started to cut herself during this time, which made her weak and light-headed. She no longer seemed to have the strength and control to keep her facade up. She would leave to go to her new job without scrubs or hospital uniforms on or any type of ID cards for her work.

This made Hann very suspicious, and he decided that he and Bich would drive Jennifer to work one night just to watch and see her go into the hospital for work. Bich even tried to follow Jennifer into the hospital after they dropped her off, but Jennifer quickly ran into the emergency department and hid from her mother.

The next morning Bich decided to call Jennifer's supposed roommate Topaz and ask her some questions. When Topaz answered the phone, she forgot the correct times that Jennifer was supposed to be there and told Bich that Jennifer wasn't there. Bich then called Jennifer on her cell phone and told her she was to come home immediately.

When Jennifer arrived home, her father made demands that she either would stay home and go to school or leave and go live with Daniel and be disowned. He told her then that she would have to wait for his death to be with Daniel again.

It now became time for damage control for Jennifer. She told her parents that it was true that she was staying at Daniel's house, and that she also lied about having a job at the hospital. But Jennifer insisted that she did attend the University of Toronto; she didn't tell her parents about not graduating from high school or not attending Ryerson University.

Jennifer did not want to leave her home, so she agreed to not see Daniel anymore. Along with not seeing Daniel, she would be grounded for two weeks and would have to go through an interrogation anytime she wanted to leave the house. Jennifer could go to her job and piano lessons and that was it. Hann made Jennifer quit her job at East Side Mario's and look for a new job because her shifts were at night and quite often she worked until 1 a.m., and this was no time for a young lady to be out.

Jennifer also had to give up her cell phone and laptop computer so that she could not communicate with others without her parents knowing. This made Jennifer panic as she thought that she might lose the affections of Daniel.

Bich became Jennifer's full-time companion now. They would spend every waking moment of the days together, leaving her no time to possibly see Daniel. After a few weeks, Jennifer managed to talk her mother into letting her check her cell phone for messages that she might have received from possible jobs.

Jennifer would now be allowed to check her messages once a day for two minutes, so it was at that time she would be able to message or even sometimes call Daniel. Jennifer would delete all her activity from her phone so that her father wouldn't see anything when he checked.

After a few months, Jennifer could use her cell phone and computer again in her parents' presence only. Jennifer was also allowed to use her mother's car now to drive herself to piano lessons, but her father would check the mileage before and after every trip.

This went okay for a brief time, but Jennifer found it difficult not to see Daniel, so she thought up a plan on how to be with him again. One night she stuffed her bed with pillows enough to make it look like she was in the bed sleeping. She then called one of her friends and had them pick her up and drive her to Daniel's house while her parents were sleeping.

The next morning Bich went into Jennifer's room to find her gone. She called her on her cell and ordered Jennifer back home immediately. Jennifer quickly came up with the story that she had just met Daniel at a coffee shop and had not gone to his house. Hann decided to send Jennifer out of province for a brief time to stay with her uncle. Upon Jennifer returning, she then told her parents that she got a job at a Walmart pharmacy, which made Hann happy, and he allowed her to use her mother's car to drive to work. Hann remembered what Jennifer had done before when she faked her job at the hospital, so he insisted on seeing a pay stub.

Jennifer quickly forged a paystub that she had found online and showed it to him. Hann then told her that he was going to drive her to work the next day. Jennifer knew that this might happen, as it did before when she was supposed to be working at the hospital. Jennifer had checked out the Walmart earlier to learn the location of the employee entrance. When they arrived at the Walmart, Jennifer walked into the Walmart and stayed there until her father left.

Hann was still not trusting Jennifer fully, so when she got home from work, he demanded to see the deposit of her Walmart paycheck into her account online. Jennifer then had to admit that she never worked at Walmart which flew Hann into a rage, calling her a liar several times.

It was at this time that Jennifer also admitted to Hann that she never went to the University of Toronto either. Hann would never be able to trust Jennifer again. Hann then made Jennifer go online with her computer and write Daniel a good-bye letter, while he watched.

Jennifer then had to apply to three colleges, one of which was Centennial College for a lab technician course, which she ended up taking. Jennifer was also grounded, just as she was before, except this time there was no time limit on it. Hann also took away her right to drive her mother's car; she was now to stay home and go to school.

The relationship between Daniel and Jennifer became strained as they could hardly talk to each other, never mind have sex. Daniel was growing tired of constantly fighting the uphill battle with Jennifer's parents, so he decided to end their relationship.

Jennifer kept sending him messages and calling his phone to try and talk to him, but he would never answer or text back to her. What Jennifer failed to realize was that there was someone new in Daniel's life.

Katrina Villanueve was a Filipino classmate of Daniel's in high school. They had never dated and were not even friends back in school. Katrina was also not liked by Daniel's parents as she had already had a child from a previous boyfriend. But Daniel liked that Katrina had lots of free time and that he didn't have to hide his relationship from people.

Daniel decided to quit University for music and started to sell drugs again. He was hanging out at the bowling alley again as Katrina loved to bowl. It was around this time that Jennifer also decided that she would move on, at least in the public eye. Jennifer would start going out with other boys and flirting with men online.

One of her new male friends was Andrew Montemayor. Jennifer had met Andrew back in elementary school when they lived in Scarborough. Andrew now worked with Jennifer's parents at Magna and lived in Mississauga with a roommate named Ricardo Duncan.

Ricardo and Andrew would brag about going to the park and robbing people at knife point, said Jennifer, but they later denied telling her that, and they were never charged for any robbery crimes. Both

Ricardo and Andrew liked Jennifer, and both wanted to sleep with her, but she didn't seem to want to be intimate with either man.

The relationship between Andrew and Jennifer is important, as it is her claim that she first contacted Andrew to get his advice on how she could deal with her father. After all, Andrew had a rough relationship with his own father at one time, but he had managed to work it out and ended up doing okay in life.

According to Jennifer, the two talked lots on Facebook Messenger where Andrew would give her advice and recommend several options to her on how to deal with her father. Andrew first told her that she might try to run away, or perhaps have someone kidnap her. Jennifer didn't like those plans as she still wanted to have a relationship with her mother.

She said that Andrew then told her about a time when he wanted to kill his own father, and this was what first made her think about how much better her life would be without her father. This seemed to create a bond between the two of them, and they would continue to discuss the subject for months to come.

Jennifer said it was all the discussions she had with Andrew that made her start to believe that her life would be better with her father dead. After all, he was the one that caused all the problems. Soon there would be a meeting that Andrew set up between Jennifer and his roommate Ric, who would be someone that could help her out with her problem.

Ric and Andrew met Jennifer at her piano school in Scarborough one night after she was finished with class. Ric was a goth-looking man, with long black hair, black nail polish and even a black hat, which surprised Jennifer as that's not what she expected Andrew's roommate to look like.

They went to a café and started to discuss Jennifer's circumstances with her father. Jennifer started by telling the two men that she wanted her father to be alone when it happened, preferably at work. She then told them that she didn't have any other thoughts and would take their advice.

It was then that Ric told her that the hit would cost her $1,300 and that he would need to find a gun. Ric then told her that he didn't have the tools to do the job yet, but when he got them, he would contact her.

It was about a week later that Ric contacted Jennifer and told her he was ready and needed to meet her to confirm the plan. The two met at a local Tim Hortons where she gave him the $1,300 and planned out the killing of her father.

According to Jennifer. the plan was going to be that Ric would go to her dad's workplace and shoot him dead in the parking lot. She then gave Ric a Google map of where her father's work was and how to get there. The two then set a date and time for the murder to happen. Jennifer then gave Ric another $200 so that he could get a gun.

After a couple of weeks went by and Jennifer had not heard from Ric, she got ahold of Andrew to ask him where Ric was. Andrew told her that Ric had moved out and he had not heard from him in a while. Jennifer realized that she had been scammed and lost her money.

Ric's version is quite different from Jennifer's. According to Ric, he met up with her with romantic intentions as he and Andrew had a bet on who could hook up with Jennifer first. Ric was able to detail the conversations that he had with her, which included her schooling and the way her dad was so hard on her.

Ric also claimed that the $200 that Jennifer had given him was so that he could go out with his friends to a karaoke bar, and there was never any plan to kill her father or buy a gun. Ric also claimed that the last time he talked to Jennifer that it was on the phone, where Jennifer asked Ric to kill both of her parents as they wouldn't let her out of the house and she was pissed off. Ric said that he thought that she was asking him only because he was black, and he told her to fuck off. It was shortly after Jennifer felt betrayed by her friends, Andrew and Ric, that she started to see Daniel again. She would start to show up at his work and visit for a few minutes,

During the past months that Daniel and Jennifer were not seeing each other, Daniel started to get weird crank phone calls or nasty text messages, all relating to threats towards Jennifer. He started to get scared and contacted Jennifer. She claimed that she had been getting them as well, and it was since he had been seeing Katrina.

So it was when they started meeting up again that the messages continued to get more intense. When the two of them went to see a movie, the text would read "why are you seeing that movie, I thought you guys were just friends, you should be with your girlfriend."

But Daniel started to get suspicious as the messages or calls would never happen when he was with Jennifer, only after. The messages always knew information that nobody else would know, like things the two of them had talked about when they were out. Even though Katrina would deny sending the messages, Jennifer continued to blame her.

The messages started to get aggressive when one day Daniel got a message saying that something was sent to Jennifer's house, and then when she opens it boom! Then the next text said Bang Bang. Daniel called Jennifer right away and told her about the message. She said a package came for her, but she didn't open it. She told him she would give it to the police.

Jennifer started to tell wild stories to Daniel, like the police were going through all her mail now and were following her around. Once she told him that the police had to take down a man who tried to switch out her water bottle in the library when she was studying.

The next event Jennifer claimed that happened to her was that when she came home from a jog, there were five Asian gang members waiting for her in her bedroom, where they raped her with her eyes covered. Jennifer also told Daniel that her mother took her to the hospital and that the police were notified and were investigating the crime.

Daniel continued to be suspicious of the rape. After all, why wouldn't it be all over the news? There had been a woman attacked in the park recently, and it was all over the news, so five Asian gang members rape a girl in her home and there wasn't a word.

So Daniel started to try and find out the truth without accusing Jennifer of anything. He would ask for trivial things such as the wrist band you get from the hospital when you've been admitted. Jennifer told him her mother took it. Another time, he asked to see her phone bill, and she would always tell him that she'd bring it next time she visited him. He thought about going to the police but, with his criminal record, he decided not to.

For some reason, Daniel stayed close to Jennifer and even professed his love for her and ignored the weird events that were happening to them.

Jennifer continued to plot the murder of her parents. After the plan with Ric fell through, she decided to suggest her plot to Daniel. Only this time she had thought through the old plan and made some changes, as she couldn't just ask Daniel to shoot her parents.

It was during a phone call with Daniel on August 16 that Jennifer first mentioned her new plan to kill her parents. It would start with a hired hitman that would break into her parents' home. During the invasion they will tie up Jennifer and her parents, then go through the house to make it look like a robbery by flipping beds, going through the drawers and demanding money of her parents who would also be tied up.

After not finding any money throughout the house, they would demand money from Jennifer, where she would give them the $2,000 that she had been saving to buy a new phone. Next the robbers would demand money from her parents, who wouldn't give them any; they would shoot them because they were infuriated, but they would leave Jennifer alive. The armed men would leave the home quickly, and Jennifer would phone 911 from her cell phone, which would be in her sweat pants.

Jennifer would remain tied up until the police arrived, she would remain helpless and scared. She would also be the only one to be interviewed as nobody else would be left alive. Sure, the plan wasn't perfect, but Jennifer believed that they were calculated risks with the lack of witnesses and evidence.

Jennifer continued to explain to Daniel that even if the detectives were suspicious, there would be no one except for her present, no contradictory information if everyone followed the plan. Jennifer didn't want this plan to fail like her first one, so Daniel set her up with a man named Homeboy. She contacted him a few times and the plans were set.

CHAPTER FOUR – TO TELL THE TRUTH

"Truth is everybody is going to hurt you, you just gotta find the ones worth suffering for." – Bob Marley

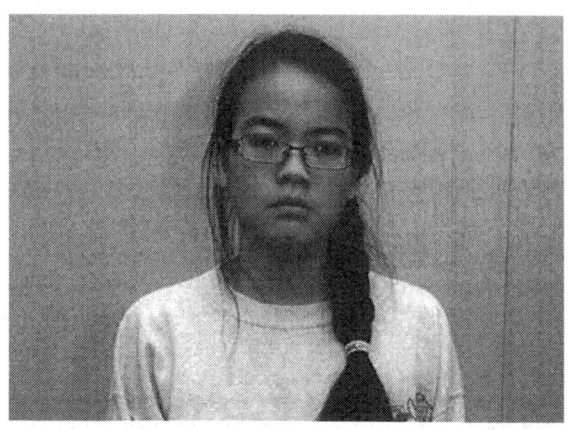

Jennifer Pan Police Picture

"My name is Jennifer Pan," she said quietly. Detective Randy Slade asked, "Can you spell that for me?" This was the beginning of a two-hour interview that was held at the Markham police station on November 9, 2010, at 2:44 A.M.

It was only about 4 hours before this interview that Jennifer Pan's family had had been attacked in their home by three male assailants. It was at about 10 pm on Monday, November 3, when the three armed men walked through the front door of the Pan family home. One pointed his gun at Bich, who had been soaking her feet while watching TV in the living room.

The other two men ran upstairs; one grabbed Jennifer and tied her hands behind her back with shoe laces, while the other burst into Hann's bedroom and put his gun into his face. Hann was then forced downstairs into the living room where Bich was being held.

The man that was holding Jennifer forced her to go into her room and give him all her money. She handed over about $2,500 to him. He then dragged her into her parents' room and demanded more money. There she brought him over to her mother's night table and gave him another $1,100 that had been stashed there.

Back in the living room, Bich had asked Hann in Cantonese how the men got into the house, and he replied that he was asleep and didn't know. The intruder that was holding a gun on them yelled at them to shut up. The intruder then focused on Hann and asked him, "Where's the fucking money?" Hann replied that he only had about $60 in his wallet.

The second intruder called Hann a liar and began to pistol whip him on the back of his head. Bich began to cry out loud and pleaded with the men not to hurt their daughter. The third intruder tied Jennifer to the arms of the upstairs banister.

Then the two assailants that had Hann and Bich took them down to the basement and covered their heads with blankets. They shot Hann, once in the shoulder and twice in the face, and he fell on the floor. They both looked at Bich, and one of them shot her three times in the head, whereupon she died instantly.

The men ran upstairs and met the third intruder, and they left out the front door.

Upstairs Jennifer managed to reach her cell phone, which had been tucked in her sweatpants, and she dialed 911. Just as the operator answered, she yelled out, "Help me, please! I don't know where my parents are! Please hurry!"

It was at the 34-second time of her call to 911 that in the background a loud moaning could be heard. It was Hann who had regained consciousness and started to crawl upstairs to the main floor. Jennifer then yelled to him that she was calling 911. Hann went outside the front door and began screaming, where a neighbor saw him and called 911 as well.

It was only minutes before the police and ambulances began to arrive at the house, and Hann was rushed to the local hospital, which in turn sent him by helicopter to a larger hospital that was a trauma center.

The York police untied Jennifer from upstairs and brought her into the detachment to conduct the interview where she would end up telling her story.

INTERVIEW ONE

Jennifer was quiet and looked down while Detective Slade went through the preliminaries of what was going to happen during the interview, as well as explain the papers that he wanted her to sign. Jennifer was obviously shattered from the terrifying events that happened earlier in the evening, so he tried to be gentle when asking her for the details.

Jennifer was wearing a sweater and sweat pants with slippers and had her hair tied in braids that hung over the front part of her body. Slade soon had her swear to tell the truth and told her of the penalty for lying under oath. She shook her head in agreement, and the interview began.

When Slade brought up that her mother Bich was murdered and that was what the interview was for, to find out any information that she could give to them to help figure out who did this, Jennifer started to cry and turn her head away. Slade gave her a tissue.

From another room behind a two-way mirror, Detective Al Cooke was watching, and the first thing that struck him as odd was when Jennifer finished her crying spell, her tissue was still dry. This was not a reliable piece of evidence as she could have been in shock.

Jennifer then began to explain how the night unfolded. A group of three assailants broke into her family home and demanded money, and when they couldn't get any from her parents, they shot them. Slade then asked her to describe the intruders.

The first man was black with a medium build and he had dreadlocks that flopped over his face so that she couldn't make out his features. She figured him to be twenty-eight to thirty-three years old, about five-and-a- half feet tall and seemed to be the one in charge. Detective Slade asked her if he had any facial hair, and she motioned her right hand around her chin saying, "I think," and paused, then finished by saying that she didn't want to say anything wrong. Jennifer called him

Number One; he had a handgun, wore black leather gloves and sounded like he was Canadian. She was quite vague about his description, telling Slade that his face was roundish and squarish.

Then she went on to describe the man she would call Number Two, who she said ran between the other two men, assisting them. He had a long, oval face and was wearing a dark hoodie and a bandana that covered his nose, and he never spoke. It seemed like Number Two just took orders and nodded when he needed to.

Jennifer then told Slade that she didn't get a good look at Number Three as he was holding her parents at gunpoint and always in a different room than where she was. She said that he had a Caribbean accent that resembled the way her high school friend's Guyanese parents spoke.

Detective Slade then asked for Jennifer to take him through the day leading up to the murder, starting with the morning of November 8. Jennifer started to explain how the day started with an odd occurrence as they were leaving the house. She and her mother noticed that the police had part of their street blocked off, and they were told that they couldn't leave due to a gas leak nearby. So they went back home, and Jennifer decided that she would stay home and practice her piano. Once the order was lifted by police, her mother left.

The rest of the day seemed to go normally, with her mother running errands and coming home for lunch. Later, her father came home from work but had to go out again to the Home Depot. Jennifer and her mother ate dinner together, and her father had his dinner a little later when he got back. After her father finished his dinner, he went into the study and read the newspaper.

Jennifer's brother, Felix, had been in Hamilton, about forty-five minutes away, where he was attending McMaster University for engineering. After supper, Jennifer's friend, Adrian Tymkewycz, dropped by and the two of them watched their favorite television shows, "How I Met Your Mother" and Gossip Girl." After that, her friend left and she went to her bedroom and watched "The Amazing Race" while talking on the phone with Edward Pacificador, who was another friend.

Jennifer heard her mother come home at 9:30 p.m. from her weekly line-dancing group that was held at a Toronto church, something her mother did every Monday. She then heard her mother rummaging around downstairs and then heard her mother yell upstairs for Hann, but she called for him in English, which she rarely did. This caused Jennifer to hang up the phone and sit in silence to listen to what was going on.

Jennifer then noticed that there were muffled voices coming from inside her home, and they were voices that she didn't recognize. This scared her. She sat for a little while until she heard all the voices leave the top floor. When it got quiet, she slowly opened her bedroom door and looked out into the hallway.

That's when she saw the man she calls Number One walking towards her, and he had string in his hands. He grabbed her abruptly and flipped her around and tied her hands up behind her back. He then told her that he had a gun on her back and to do what he tells her and she won't get hurt. He wanted her to show him the money.

Jennifer said that she showed him where she kept $2,000 in cash, which she had been saving to buy the new iPhone. Then the man forced her to her parents' bedroom, which was across the hall from hers. This time, both Number One and Number Two men asked her where her parents kept their money. She told them that she didn't know, and the men ransacked the room, flipping the bed and pulling out the drawers where some money fell out.

The two men now dragged Jennifer down the stairs and ordered her to kneel on the floor and keep her eyes facing the ground. She could hear the Number Three man yelling at her mother, demanding her wallet. She said her mother kept trying to get up, but they kept telling her to sit down. They were trying to find her wallet, but her mother didn't speak good English; she stood up one last time, and they shoved her back onto the couch.

Jennifer said that she didn't want her mother to get hurt, so she told her to sit down, and then Jennifer begins to sob uncontrollably. Detective Slade told her to take her time, all of this is very important, so take your time. Hann then told the men that he had a wallet upstairs with $60 in it, so the men grabbed Jennifer from the floor and dragged her upstairs to get the wallet.

As soon as the men found the money, Number One asked Number Two to get a string from "Cuzy" and Number Two left for a couple of minutes. When Number Two returned, he had a string which he used to tie Jennifer to the upstairs banister.

The men went downstairs, and the next thing Jennifer remembers is hearing the men take her parents down to the basement. It was a few minutes later that she could hear one of the men yelling, "You lied, you lied to us!" Then she heard two pops and her mother screamed, which made Jennifer yell out to her, then she heard a couple of more pops. Jennifer then heard her mother moan and then one more pop, and one of the guys yelled out, "We have to go now, it's been too long." And then she heard them run out the front door.

Jennifer then was able to get to her phone to call the police and could now hear her father coming up the stairs from the basement. She still hadn't heard anything from her mother. All she could hear was her father running out the front door yelling.

Jennifer now finished her story, and Detective Slade asked her to go through the account of events one more time, but this time he wanted her to describe the events as if she was a character looking down at what she saw. This was to not only help her remember what happened, but it also is an opportunity to catch any variances in the story.

When Jennifer started telling her second version of the story, there ended up being some key differences, first when she said when her mother came home, she didn't see her. In the second telling, she claimed that she went downstairs to greet her mother.

Also in her first account, one of the intruders came at her with a string, but in the second account, she claimed that Number One showed her his gun which was in his holster before demanding that she sit down on the bed, then he grabbed the money, which now became $2,500 instead of $2,000. In the second version, Jennifer told Slade that she wasn't tied up until Number Two brought a shoelace.

Next when she was brought downstairs she said that the men told her to sit, rather than kneel. In the second telling, she also added that she never kept her eyes aimed at the floor, but disobeyed the men's order and looked up to see Number Three. She was now able to describe Number Three as a man with a thin build, and he was pointing his gun at her father.

Another key difference was that the men had found $1,100 of American money, which her parents had out for a planned trip to the States, and this time the men did not find Hamm's wallet and kept yelling at her father for not co-operating with them.

In the second recall of events, Jennifer said that she heard the men taking her parents into the basement, but this time heard her mother calling for her, saying that she wanted her daughter. Then she heard the first two pops and her mother screamed, and Jennifer yelled out for her mother, then there were two more pops, then she heard her mother say something else, and one final pop, and then the men ran out the door.

It was a few minutes after that when Jennifer was able to call 911. She then recalls hearing her dad groaning and leaving the house. She said that she yelled to him, but he wouldn't come back inside; he was trying to get help, she figured.

That ended up being a point that the detectives couldn't get out of their minds, as why would her injured father leave the house, knowing that his daughter was still inside the house and not try to save her? He would have heard her screaming and did not try to go to her, instead just left the house.

The questions then turned to Jennifer about her own situation with work and school. Detective Slade wanted to know about how Jennifer got so much money to purchase a new iPhone, and she told him that she earned her money from giving piano lessons. He then asked her about her education, and she only mentioned that she was planning to go back to school in January to study biotechnology engineering.

Slade finished by asking her if there was anything strange that happened before the murder, and she told him that they lived a straightforward, almost routine life. He then mentioned to her that her brother, Felix, was being interviewed in the next room, which clearly agitated her. She asked why Felix had to be interviewed, and Slade answered that it was more of an administration; after all, you never know.

Slade then left the room, and Jennifer was left alone except for the video camera which was recording her. She took a gulp from a bottled water that was brought to her before the interview started, and then placed her head in her hands. Eventually she sat up and moved her hands over her stomach.

Next, she shakily stood up, seemingly not being able to get her balance and leaning against the wall. Once she got stable, she started to walk around the room, always with one hand touching the wall. She would shake her hands and place her head face first against the wall.

Slade returned to the room about twenty minutes later and the two of them sat down. Slade began to tell her that it doesn't take a rocket scientist to figure out that the intruders might have been drawn to her mother because of the type of car she was driving and where she was driving to; "It's something we have to explore."

Jennifer then came to attention telling Slade that her mother did drive a Lexus and her father drove a Mercedes, and the family had wealthy aesthetics. The excitement in Jennifer's voice changed drastically when Slade brought up her electronic communication and told her that they had been time-stamping her data usage from her cellphone.

Jennifer then blurted out, "I just don't, like, I talk to people on the phone, but I don't..." Then Slade interrupted her with, "The unfortunate thing is that Edward and Adrian are probably going to be interviewed because they were in the house and on the phone with you."

Slade continued to explain to Jennifer that the media is going to be around this case, and that the police have no control over what they say or do; his advice to her was to turn the TV off. Home invasion type robberies where someone is murdered can become very big news.

Slade then presented her with a consent form for her to sign giving the police permission to access all her calls and texts from her Rogers Samsung phone between November 1 and 8. While she signed the document, she asked who would be contacted and how deep into this would they look, saying that she was concerned about people like her piano teachers and stuff like that.

Slade then explained how vital cellphone records were in today's world, and in murder cases, it helps them to confirm where the people involved were from tower pings. It would firm up your story, so say you say that you were in your room when you received a certain phone call, this will show up on the tower site information.

It also may turn out that you were targeted in your area, and would allow us to go back and look for cameras in those areas. Not saying that it's going to happen in your case, but if you're lying as part of this whole process, telling us fictitious information, now the records can be used against you.

Jennifer then wanted to know if they would tell her who is contacted on her phone, but Slade didn't respond. She then left the police station; it was about 5:00 a.m.

It was around this time the detectives learned of Hann being put into an induced coma and the possibility that he might not make it.

CHAPTER FIVE – IVE GOT A SECRET

"The secret to happiness is freedom, and the secret to freedom is courage." - Thucydides

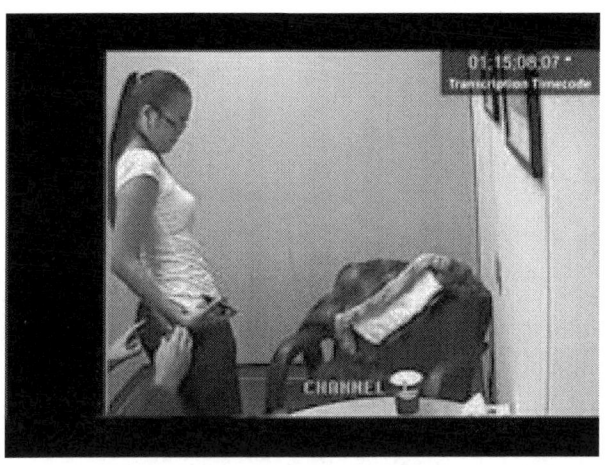

Jennifer demonstrating how she phoned 911

The media soon descended on the Pan house and police station to report all the details. There was an instant fear in the town of Markham as it appeared to be a home invasion where two innocent people had been shot.

The police had a public news conference to try and ease some of the people in the community.

The murderers may have been attracted to the home because of the family's high-end vehicles; however, they noted that neither vehicle was taken as part of the robbery. The police also wouldn't let the public know how much money was taken in the home invasion or that there was still money in Hann's wallet, Bich's purse and Jennifer's room. They also said that there was no sign of forced entry into the home suggesting that the door was unlocked.

They released a description of the three assailants which was according to Jennifer's statement;

Number One — male, black, twenty-eight to thirty-three years old, five feet, seven inches tall with a medium build.

Number Two – male, black, thirty-one years old, five feet, eight inches tall, with a thin build, wearing a dark hood and a bandana over his face.

Number Three – male, thin build, with a Caribbean accent.

It was about 10 a.m. when Jennifer and a lot of her family all were at the intensive care unit at the Toronto Sunnybrook Hospital praying for her father. One bullet had entered Hann's face and travelled down to his neck where it was still lodged. There were also still bullet fragments in his face. The bullet missed a vital artery and it looked like he would come out of it alive.

It was outside of the Pan family home that two police detectives sat in their command post RV where they were plotting their course for canvassing the neighborhood, when a young man knocked on their door. The man told the detectives that Jennifer's boyfriend, Daniel Wong, was a drug dealer and that she was his delivery person. One of the officers ran a check on Daniel and found that he had been convicted of selling drugs a few years before. They then set up an interview with Daniel Wong for the next day at 4 p.m.

Daniel walked into the Markham police detachment with his girlfriend, Katrina Villanueva. He had a cold and was constantly sniffing. When Detective Robert Milligan came into the room to interview him, the first thing that he noticed was that Daniel was calm, polite and very friendly. In fact, when Milligan left the room for a few minutes, Daniel fell asleep with his head on the table.

Milligan and Wong got along well from the start while Daniel talked about his life, from his job at Boston Pizza to attending York University. The topic then changed to whether Daniel had a girlfriend, and he replied that it was Katrina, the woman that came with him to the interview.

Milligan then asked him about his relationship with Jennifer. Daniel told him that she was his ex-girlfriend and they had dated from high school until about two years ago. He then went on to explain that they were together a total of seven years, and that it was all behind the backs of her parents.

Daniel then told Milligan of all the weird behavior that Jennifer displayed, when she had her parents believing that she was attending University to become a pharmacist, when in fact she wasn't. She would spend three nights a week at his family's home in East Toronto while her parents thought that she was staying at her girlfriend Topaz's apartment.

Daniel admitted that they had planned to get married, but he knew in the back of his mind that he had never been liked by her parents. He wasn't even allowed to call her at home. He figured that her parents never thought that he was good enough for Jennifer and couldn't make enough money working at Boston Pizza to give her a good life. Jennifer's parents also took issue with his ethnicity, as he was only half Chinese and was half Filipino.

Daniel then told Milligan that her parents told Jennifer that she had to choose between them and Daniel. She then quit her jobs, stopped seeing him, and stayed at home. Her cellphone and laptop were taken from her as well, so they had no real way of talking. This is what ended their relationship.

It was from that point on that they never really spoke again. Occasionally they would visit or have the odd phone call, but it was superficial and nothing important was ever said.

The conversation was then aimed at her parents. Daniel told the detective that he had only ever been invited to her house once to meet the parents, so he didn't get to know anything about them. Anything that he could tell Milligan about them had come from Jennifer.

From what she had told Daniel, her parents never slept in the same bed -- her mother would always sleep in the basement. They would often be fighting, and her mother did all the work around the house, while her father took them for granted. Daniel also told the detective about the home renovation the family had just done that cost them about $30,000.

Milligan switched the topic again to Daniel's run-in with the law. He right away denied that her parents knew anything about his convictions for drugs, and his second arrest was not his fault because a friend of his borrowed Daniel's car and was pulled over and charged with possession. What Detective Milligan wanted to know if Jennifer was involved in his drug dealings. Daniel denied that she ever touched the stuff and said he didn't want her to get involved in it either.

It was then that the detective asked Daniel about all the bizarre communications that he had received since the break-up by text and phone. Daniel started by saying that it had increased lately where somebody would call, and he'd answer, and it would be quiet for about ten seconds, then they would hang up. It could be a hundred times a night.

Daniel then started getting text messages that were threatening, like "Ha, Bang." But he then said that Jennifer was getting these same types of phone calls, too, only hers were calling her stupid and ugly and questioned why Daniel would ever want to date a girl like her. His new girlfriend Katrina was receiving these types of phone calls as well.

Things really got scary when Jennifer received a bullet in the mail, and then she was raped by five Asian gang members. Milligan then asked if Daniel's drug clientele might have done the home invasion and killed Jennifer's mother. Daniel responded by saying that he was more than 95 to 99 percent sure that it had nothing to do with his drug dealing as he sold marijuana, and nobody is going to shoot you for that. It was Daniel's opinion that it had something to do with the crank calls.

At the end of the interview, Milligan then asked Daniel what it would cost to have someone taken out and what would he charge to kill somebody, give me a number. Daniel's response was that if someone was desperate enough, they'll do it for any amount, but it would probably have to be around $10,000. That ended the two-hour interview, and Daniel left the police station.

CHAPTER SIX - THE NEXT IN LINE

"When someone shows you who they are, believe them the first time." – Maya Angelou

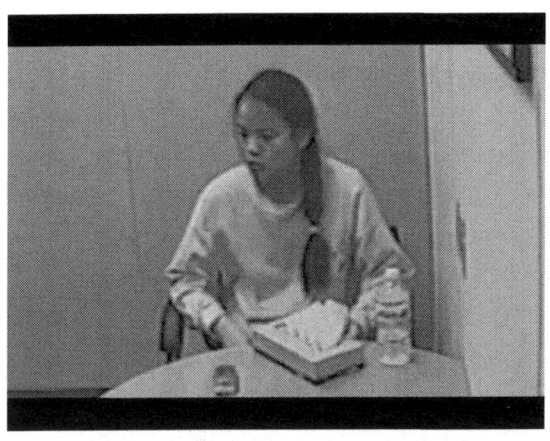

Jennifer Pan during interview

On November 11 at about 9:45 a.m., Jennifer arrived at the Markham Police station to have her second interview, where she appeared to be scared and very shaky. It started out just as the first interview had, with the detective swearing her in to tell the truth, and she agreed. Slade then asked her if she had suffered from any mental illness or had been drinking or took any drugs. She curiously only answered that she did no drugs or no drinking.

Jennifer then stated that she was very nervous and didn't want to say the wrong thing, as bits and pieces of what happened that day are here, while other pieces are not. Slade confidently replied to her that the truth is always the best way to relieve her anxiety.

Slade then asked her what exactly happened on the night of November 8 again as he had multiple questions about her first interview with him. During her retelling of the events that happened that night, again there were several differences from her first interview.

This time she explained how she was sitting on her bed frozen when she heard her mother call up to her father in Vietnamese. In her first interview, she said that her mother called up in English which is what scared her. Jennifer then recounted that when she looked out her door, she saw Number One coming at her with his gun drawn and in his hand. In the first interview, she said that he came at her with string in his hands.

Jennifer then continued with her story but failed to mention the $1,100 that was taken from her parents' room, saying that she didn't see them recover anything. Slade then stopped her and asked if she was sure, because the first time that they talked, she had mentioned there was some money taken. She then claimed that it was a couple of hundred American dollars that was taken.

Next came a question of why she thought that the intruders didn't ask for the combination for the safe that was in her parents' room and not hidden from sight. When Jennifer was unable to answer, Slade then asked her about a second phone that she had. Jennifer went on to tell him that her friend Daniel gave it to her so that she could talk to him without detection from her father. She couldn't remember the last time she used the phone, but she hadn't talked to Daniel in weeks.

Slade then asked Jennifer to stand up and show him how she was able to call 911 on her cellphone with her hands tied behind her back. This was only the first question that the police had concerning the cellphone. How did the phone stay lodged in Jennifer's sweat pants without falling out after being dragged and pushed around the house, up and down stairs, and how was it not seen by the intruders?

Jennifer nodded her head, then drank some water before she took her sweater off and stood up slowly; she seemed to be trying to delay the display that she was asked to do. She picked up the fake cellphone that the police placed in front of her and placed it in her waistband.

Jennifer then placed her hands behind her back as if they had been tied with string. She then bent her head around facing her back and looking towards the phone. She pulled the phone out of her waistband and directed it towards her face, and just then Slade asked her how she made the phone call.

The phone was about two feet from her face and she pretended to talk into the phone as if she was talking to the 911 operator. Slade then wanted to know how she could hear the operator with her ear being so far away from the phone. She responded by telling him that she had turned the volume up as high as it would go.

After Jennifer demonstrated how she made the phone call, she became distant to Detective Slade and refused to let him help her get her sweater back on. He offered her some more water and she quietly refused. Even though Jennifer appeared to be really upset with the interview, Slade decided to turn up the volume on her next.

The detective asked Jennifer to recount the events of that evening one more time, except this time he wanted her to go backwards. It was a great struggle for her to go through the story as she kept pausing. While she was holding her stomach like she was in great pain, he asked if everything was okay. Slade then left the room and gave her a break.

When the detective returned to the room, he immediately asked Jennifer if she could tell him about her relationship with Daniel and how they were able to keep it from her parents for so long. She responded by saying that it just happened, and she wasn't allowed to have boyfriends, so didn't get to see him that much.

Jennifer slowly got into her fake university and how it was all because of her father, who wanted her to be a doctor or pharmacist. So Slade asked her what she did with her time while she was pretending to go to school or work. She then told the detective that she just lied to him and would go to the library and would make up term papers as if she had been attending school.

Jennifer then explained how her parents had such high expectations of her that she couldn't tell them the truth. She then asked if Slade would not tell her father that she never really attended any university and didn't even finish high school. She also tried to explain that her life had become nothing but waking up, playing piano, helping with chores, going to her music lessons, and returning home again.

Slade then asked Jennifer if she resented her parents for all of this, and she responded by telling him that she chose what she chose, and she chose her family.

Detective Slade then wanted her to tell him about Daniel's drug dealings, and she told him that she was never involved. The question then went to her father and if he had any involvement in drugs or gambling, to which she said that she didn't think so.

Jennifer then told the detective about how her father was having an affair with a Chinese-speaking woman and she had heard the two of them on the phone once, and he would leave, telling her that he was going over to her cousin's house to help her with homework. But later when Jennifer had asked her cousin, she found out that her father had come over, but much later than when he left home. Jennifer said that this was the first time she caught her father in a lie.

After a half-hour break, Slade returned to the interview room and this time told Jennifer how the media was portraying this as a drug-related murder and break-in, and he wanted to know if she thought that she had been mistaken somehow of being involved with Daniel's life in dealing. She quickly shook her head no without saying a word.

Next Slade once again asked her if she had any involvement in what happened, or in anything illegal that would have drawn attention to her that would bring bad people to her house looking for large amounts of money. Again, she didn't speak and only shook her head no.

Slade continued by stating that it was unusual for the intruders to have left Jennifer upstairs alone and not to have done to her what they did to her parents. Jennifer continued to keep shaking her head no and then finally spoke, saying that the only thing she could think of was that she was cooperating with the intruders.

Slade then forcefully told her that she lied to her parents and how does he know that she wasn't telling him a lie, too. This silenced Jennifer and she lowered her head again and started shaking her head no again. "This wasn't an evil plot that you thought of?" he said strongly. "Oh, my God, no!" she said. "You didn't have anything to do with this whatsoever?" Slade asked, and she quickly responded, "No."

After a few minutes, Slade then asked her if there was anything in her account that she wanted to change, and she told him that she felt like she said something wrong. Slade asked her if she could be lying to him, and she told him that she couldn't because he was scaring her.

It was 2 p.m. and the four-hour interview was now over, and Jennifer left the police station.

CHAPTER SEVEN – COMING BACK FROM THE DEAD

"Death is not the greatest loss in life. The greatest loss is what dies inside us while we live." – Norman Cousins

Hann Pan Jennifer's father

It was on November 12 that Hann came out of his coma but was still in a great deal of pain as he had a bullet still lodged in his neck and was unable to breathe without a device that was attached to his mouth. He was still suffering from the fragments of the bullet in his face and he was unable to speak.

Hann could have family members around him to comfort him from the murder of his wife and the events that tore his family apart that evening. Jennifer was not allowed to talk with him or see him until the police finished with all their interviews.

The next day, the two police detectives arrived at Hann's hospital room to start their interview with him. The first question that one of the officers asked was if he remembered what had happened that night. Hann started by telling them that two black men and one white man broke into his home.

When asked to describe his assailants, he said that they were all about six feet tall and wore black clothing that seemed to have brown splotches all over them. You could see that it was very painful for him to talk, but he completed his description of the three men as well as he could.

Hann then told the detectives that his daughter Jennifer was free to walk around the house while the intruders were terrorizing him and his wife. They then had a conversation that focused on Jennifer, but Hann told them it was most important to find those that were responsible. The detectives assured him that they would solve the case and left his room.

Hann specifically told his family that he did not want to see his daughter Jennifer, but on January 13, after the police finished with the interview, she managed to sneak into his room. Hann did not accuse her of being involved but asked her if she thought that Daniel was behind the break-in. She told him that she didn't think that Daniel could do anything like that. It was then that Jennifer asked her dad for $1,200 for her tuition.

It was on November 15 that the family had Bich's funeral. Both Jennifer and her brother Felix were there, but their father was still too ill and in the hospital, so he couldn't attend.

CHAPTER EIGHT – WHAT HAPPENS TO ME?

"My father gave me the greatest gift anyone could give another person, he believed in me." – Jim Valvano

Daniel Wong

The third interview started on November 22 at 2 p.m. after the police paid for a taxi to pick Jennifer up and bring her to the police station. She was taken into the interview room where she remained standing while she waited for the detective to show up. Soon after, a large, stocky man with grey hair cut in a military style entered the room. It was not Detective Slade who she had in the previous two interviews.

The man sat down and told her his name was Detective Goetz. He made it clear that he was not in the mood for her diversions and asked her if she knew why they were here today. Jennifer, now at attention, sat down across from the man and reluctantly replied, "To discuss stuff?" "Regarding what?" he abruptly responded to her.

There was a short pause and Jennifer looked towards the ground before she slowly answered, "About what happened at my home." Loudly Goetz said, "As a result of that home invasion, your father was shot, and your mother Bich-Ha was killed, is that correct?" With her eyes still facing downwards, she nodded.

"You'll have to speak up!" Goetz exclaimed. 'Sorry, yes," she replied, and now she was wiping her eyes as if she was crying. The detective offered her no tissue or sympathy. Realizing now that the recording equipment was no longer working, Goetz told her that they would have to change rooms. She asked him not to leave her alone, and the detective just snapped back at her, "Hold on."

They got into the new room and both sat down, and right away Detective Goetz started by saying, "If you had any involvement in that home invasion, then you could be facing charges of murder and attempted murder. Anything you do say to us regarding that home invasion is being recorded and could be used as evidence in court. You understand that?" Jennifer quietly responded, "Yes."

After this initial bad cop treatment, Goetz then became good cop, as he leaned back in his chair and asked her about her love for music, the piano, and figure skating. Jennifer started to come around, looked up at him, and started to talk about the things that she loved.

Detective Goetz even told her about the time when he tried playing piano and made her laugh when he called the ballet "Swan Lake" "Swan of the lake." The two of them seemed to be getting along great; he had even laughed a few times.

Jennifer then began talking about her parents always comparing her to her classmates, teammates, and cousins and, in fact, she felt so much pressure from her parents that she had to forge her high school report cards to hide her average grades from them.

She went on to tell Goetz that it wasn't just her transcripts that she lied to her parents about, but also the man she was dating, Daniel. Jennifer felt that she had to hide it from her parents as they didn't allow her to have boyfriends. Once her parents found out she had been dating Daniel, they demanded that she not see him again because they didn't like that he was of mixed race.

Jennifer then said that she made the choice of her family over Daniel, and her parents were probably right, as Daniel moved on to another woman named Katrina. This made her feel very unwanted and led to her cutting herself and attempting suicide, which she kept from everybody.

It was at this point the detective told Jennifer that her parents' expectations were too high and that it was a form of abuse. Goetz then brought up that she had thought that the intruders liked her and that's probably why they kept her alive. Jennifer then added that she had asked the intruders why she couldn't be with her parents and they told her because she cooperated.

Goetz then asked her how many African-Canadian males she knew and told her that the police had a photo of her sitting with a black man in a café. Jennifer told him that the man in the café was Ric, who was a roommate of a friend, and that she lent him money once to help pay his rent.

Out of the blue, Goetz then asked Jennifer directly if she thought that it made sense that, if the intruders were going to kill your parents, that they would leave a witness alive, or do you think that they just made a mistake? She then told him that she thought they were just running out of time and had to go before they got caught. Goetz then got up and left the room.

Goetz came back into the room and sat down and looked directly into Jennifer's eyes and started to talk. "We have computer programs, we feed everything into the computer and it analyzes what a person has said. It tells us where the areas of deception are, areas of concern, and areas that are flat-out not truthful. You come back with results that say not possible. Do you watch CSI at all?" "A little," she softly answered.

"The police are going over that house with a fine-tooth comb. They're going over every hair fiber, every skin cell, every bit of blood. You know what DNA is, right? A person cannot go in or out of anywhere without leaving a part of themselves behind. Your doorknob is very important. We're looking for who was the last one who touched that door lock. We would get fingerprints of one person locking it and then overlapped by the person that unlocked it.

"Another thing we utilize is satellites. The satellite is a twenty-four-hour video that's going on. It's recording information. The military uses it for precision bombing. We're able to go back and review that. It's like an X-ray. We're able to tell, are people in the positions that the witness is telling us they were in or are they different? Another thing we do is talk to a lot of people. We don't leave any rock unturned. You've heard of CrimeStoppers, right? When you get a case like this, people want to help. It's in the papers, it's everywhere. So, people end up coming to us to help us out with the case. Three people are inside the house. Somebody always tells somebody else. Suddenly, we get people calling in. They want to help. You don't know how many people call in on their friends. They want money. They get greedy."

Goetz continued for almost an hour non-stop, not letting Jennifer say anything. "Nothing surprises me in this job. I am well aware that anyone on this Earth is capable of making a mistake." Just then she bowed her head towards the ground again. "I don't care if they're a priest or a schoolteacher. One thing that you must remember is that your dad was there, and your dad had a front row seat to all of this. Your dad's a very smart man and he had a very clear perception of what's going on. A lot of the things you told the police didn't happen. It doesn't match at all.

"You've spent a considerable amount of time over the past seven years telling half-truths, and I can understand why. You've had a tough life. What's

74

happened to you, to me equates to abuse. Now you're under a tremendous amount of stress. You're involved in this. I know that. You've lived your whole life trying to live up to expectations that you can't make. You're a twenty-four-year-old woman being treated like a fifteen-year-old. You're not the first person to lie about dating a guy, because in your culture they don't accept it. Who else is involved in this?"

"I don't know," Jennifer answers. "We know that you were involved, but we also know that you're a good person that's made a mistake here," Goetz continued. "You got involved with the wrong people. You don't want to keep living this lie. Everyone knows, and you're getting that feeling. Nobody is surprised here. You were a prisoner in your own house. You were living someone else's expectations. No matter how much they love you, they're taking away Jen. The Jen that just wanted to be a piano teacher. Why is that not good enough? Why not just be a lab technician? Why a doctor? Why does it always have to be something bigger?"

Jennifer remained quiet with her hands on her lap and her head facing the floor. Goetz continued, "At some point, even the nicest dog, when it's cornered, bites back. It's called self-preservation. Eighteen months ago, you chose your family over Daniel, but you gave up Jen. Jen was in a state of depression, backed into a corner. Why you froze there on your bed was because the plan was in motion, there was no turning back. And I know right now you wish you could turn it back, right?

"It was a form of abuse," Goetz kept going. "You can't do that to a person. This is Canada. We're in the twenty-first century here. It's like your dad fixing everybody else's home but not his own. It's the same with you. He was trying to make a future for you bigger than it should have been. In the process of his love for you, he made the mistake of pushing you away. All his good intentions went the other way. The good thing is that you didn't shoot anyone here. You couldn't do that. You're not that type of person, right?"

Still sitting silent with her face still not looking at the detective, Goetz then wheeled his chair so that he was only inches away from Jennifer now. He looked at her intently and said, "You're involved in this, I know that. There's no question about it. The only question right now is, are you going to keep making mistakes?" It was now about three hours into the interview, and Jennifer finally looked up at Goetz and said, "What happens to me?"

CHAPTER NINE - IS THAT WHAT I SAID?

"I am whatever you say I am, if I wasn't, then why would you say I am." - Eminem

Jennifer and her brother Felix Pan

Jennifer then repeated it two more times, "What happens to me?" before detective Goetz finally answered, "I don't know the details, so I can't even say. We're going to have to deal with this one step at a time. You've got to be honest with me, and then you and I are going to work through this together. But I need to hear it."

Jennifer then began to talk, "I wanted it to stop." Goetz then said, "I know you did. Once they came in, you couldn't stop it, could ya?" "I didn't know who they were," Jennifer answered. "Are you sorry for what happened? Do you wish you could take it back?" Goetz asked her. Jennifer then said, "Yes."

"That's good, that's positive. You wish it didn't happen," Goetz said as he started to rub her back. "I know this has been hell for you. All you were looking for is a break, a chance to be on your own, to make your own decisions. How did it start? What was your plan? We know you were involved from the start. Over three hundred kids in North America every year are involved in their parents' death. And when we consider those cases, there's always a common factor. In those cases, those kids had to live up to expectations. The house rules were just so out of whack."

Jennifer spoke up, "If I could have stopped it, I would have stopped it." Again she put her face into her hands. "They were supposed to take me." Goetz quickly responded, "They were supposed to take you? Why? They were supposed to take the whole family out?" "No, just me, because I didn't want to be here anymore. I'm such a disappointment."

"It wasn't supposed to be your mom, is that what you're telling me? What about your dad?" Goetz quickly asked. "It was supposed to be me, so they could be free from me. I was a disappointment in everything, even when I tried suicide I failed." "Who did you get to do this then?" Goetz asked. "I don't know who he is. I just got his number," Jennifer says. "The order was to come in and take me out. I was the only girl in the house."

Jennifer then told Goetz that she got the number for a man that was called 'Homeboy' from her roommate's friend Ric. About two months before the home invasion, she contacted Homeboy and they made their plans. Homeboy told her that she would need to have the money in cash to give to the men when they got to the house that night. She then told him that she would get a text that night before the men arrived saying "Game on."

Goetz then looked at Jennifer and asked her to sit up and to look him in the eyes and started to say, "What you've just told me is half-truth. What I believe is that you went to somebody, and I do believe that night you paid them the $2,000. That's the true part. But what's not true is that it was never for you. The job was for your parents.

"Your dad wasn't supposed to live, but when he did live, he was able to tell us what happened that night, which conflicted with what you told us," Goetz said. "This is how you deal with stress. You give half and you keep half. That's your stress mechanism. That's what you've been trained to do. No one thinks bad of you here; everybody in the police department feels sorry for you. Basically it's like a volcano, and at one point it was just too much and you erupted."

Jennifer came back quickly, "Is that what you want me to say? But that's not what happened." The two of them went back and forth like this for about another half hour, then Goetz, who was completely frustrated, got up and left the room.

A few minutes later, Goetz came back into the interview room but now totally calm. He sat down and said "I need you to listen close, okay, Jen? At this point of the investigation, I will be arresting you for murder, also attempted murder and conspiracy to commit murder. Do you understand?" Jennifer looked down at the floor again, covered her ears and started to cry.

Goetz then said with authority, "You have to listen, so can you take your hands off your ears? Do you have anything to say in response to the charges?" Jennifer now looked up and shakily said, "I thought you were on my side." Goetz then went in and out of the room several more times getting all the paperwork ready for the charges.

It was on November 23, 2010, at 3:30 p.m. that Armand La Barge, Chief of the York Region police, held a news conference in Markham, where he announced the arrest of 24-year-old Jennifer Pan for murder, attempted murder and conspiracy to commit murder.

Detective Sergeant Larry Wilson, the lead investigator, also speaking at the news conference, spoke next saying that Jennifer had been arrested the night before and appeared in court earlier that morning for a bail hearing, is still in custody, and will be back in court again on November 30.

La Barge then cautioned that police are still seeking three other suspects for the November 8 incident that occurred at the Markham, Ontario, home of Bich Ha and Huei Hann Pan, where at about 10 p.m. three armed suspects are believed to have entered the 238 Helen Avenue home where the Pans lived with Jennifer. He noted that their son is attending university in Hamilton and was not home at the time.

For reasons that are not yet known, the suspects shot both Bich Ha and Huei Hann multiple times while ransacking the house. The suspects allegedly tied up the daughter and left her upstairs. Paramedics pronounced the 53-year old woman dead at the scene. Her 57-year-old husband stumbled to a neighbor's home for help. Jennifer allegedly told police she freed herself. She called 911 about 10:30 p.m. Huei Hann has since been released from hospital and is recovering in a place of safety.

Wilson said that Huei Hann is aware that his daughter has been charged. Wilson then said the investigation changed direction in roughly the past week after it became clear that Jennifer's and Huei's descriptions of the suspects didn't match up. Police are not prepared to talk about any possible motive at this time. No allegations against Jennifer Pan have been proven in a court of law.

La Barge said the investigation remains active, and that police are seeking three individuals:

Suspect 1 – black male, 20-25 years old, 6'2", muscular build

Suspect 2 – black male, 20-25 years old, 6'2", skinnier build than Suspect 1

Suspect 3 – white male, 20-25 years old, 6' with heavier build and a round face.

La Barge said the three remaining suspects should be considered armed and extremely dangerous. "I'm strongly urging these three men to retain counsel and to surrender themselves to police immediately." La Barge then asked anyone with information about the crime to contact police or CrimeStoppers.

For the police, the easy part was over. Now it was going to be the long and arduous process of not only finding the three assailants that murdered Bich Ha Pan, but also proving that the men were responsible.

CHAPTER TEN – FACE THE MUSIC

"Courage is resistance to fear, mastery of fear, not absence of fear." – Mark Twain

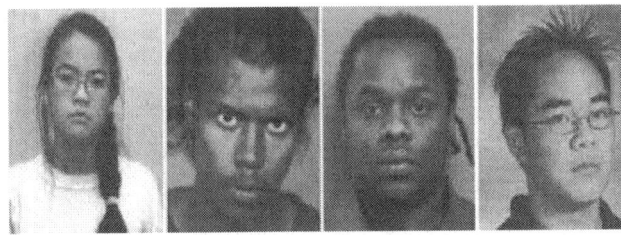

Jennifer Pan, David Mylvaganam, Eric Carty, Daniel Wong

On November 25, just after Jennifer was arrested, the police received the call logs from Jennifer's iPhone. The first thing that stuck out was that there were calls between Daniel and Jennifer. In fact, there were 36 text messages and 14 phone calls between the two of them, even though Daniel told cops that the two of them never talked anymore.

The next thing police found was that there were several phone calls and texts from prepaid cell phones, so there was no information on who owned the phones; you could just buy them at a store for a certain amount of money and they had a limited time on them to make calls and texts, and once the time is used up, you throw away the phone.

The police then decided that they would focus on the phone calls that Jennifer received on the day of the murder. The home invasion occurred at 10:13 p.m. and the last call she had was just five minutes before that at 10:03 p.m. which only lasted for 3 minutes and 33 seconds.

There were three other calls that night, at 6:12 p.m., 8:16 p.m., and 9:34 p.m., and all three of them were short, under two minutes long. The police obtained a warrant for the records of these phones as well as the ping information from the towers that these phones used.

The police then decided to call and text each of the phones to see if they got an answer. All phones were silent except for one, the number that phoned Jennifer at 8:16 p.m. the night of the murder. The name of the owner, which was fake, was James Anderson; his name was really **Demetrius Mables**, who the police brought in for questioning later that day.

When asked about the phone call from his phone to Jennifer the day of the murder, he denied calling her. He also had an alibi for that night as he was working at a construction site so couldn't have been involved.

Detectives then found one of the numbers registered to a real address; it was the number that called Jennifer twice on the date of the murder, at 10:00 a.m. and 6:12 p.m. It ended up belonging to the house of **Lenford Crawford** and his parents. When the police arrived at Crawford's house, they woke him up and took him in for questioning.

Crawford was first asked if he knew **Daniel Wong**, to which he replied that he used to hang out with him years ago. Detectives then asked Crawford how he knew Jennifer Pan, to which he at first denied knowing her, then admitted to calling her because he was looking for Daniel. When asked why he was looking for Daniel that morning, Crawford told them that Daniel's friend Vince had owed Crawford $500 and he wanted it back.

After the interview ended with Crawford, police checked out the work alibi that both Crawford and Daniel had given for the night of the home invasion, and it checked out, as both were at work that evening until midnight.

The police would keep watch over the three suspects as they didn't feel comfortable with any of them and the stories they had about calling Jennifer. So police started looking through Jennifer's second phone, a Samsung Galaxy, which was the phone she used for work and piano lessons. There was a person that called and texted her a lot the day of the home invasion, **Andrew Montemayor**, so they brought him in for questioning.

Detective Goetz asked Andrew about why he phoned Jennifer the day of the murder, and Andrew told the detective that he didn't call her. Goetz then slammed a stack of papers on the desk in front of Andrew and said that they were the records proving that Andrew texted Jennifer 86 times and called her four times that day.

Faced with the evidence of the texts and calls that he had made to Jennifer, Andrew started to talk. He told the detective that Jennifer had communicated with him to complain about her parents and feeling like she was under house arrest. Jennifer then told Andrew that she had planned a home invasion at her house for later that night which was going to look like a robbery.

Jennifer described what was going to happen in the home invasion in detail, where it would start by two men breaking into the house and demanding money. She would be tied up but not hurt and would decide what was to happen that night.

Andrew then explained that Jennifer had asked him before, in 2010, if he could help her to kill her parents. She was really upset by the way her father was treating her and how much her parents didn't trust her.

Police then conducted a photo line-up with Hann Pan at the Markham police detachment on January 6. Hann took a seat and started to go through the series of pictures slowly, and on the fifth photo, he stopped, then framed the face with his fingers. He sat quietly for a few minutes before he told the police that he thought that was one of the men; he was not 100 percent sure, but he thinks it's him. The picture was of **David Mylvaganam**.

The next interview the detectives had was with the man named Ric, who Jennifer said had given her the contact info for 'Homeboy,' who was supposed to have been the one who set up the home invasion for Jennifer.

Ric claimed that he had met Jennifer through his room-mate Andrew, who was a friend of hers. The two became friends and would text and phone each other a lot. They met for coffee a couple of times, but when Jennifer started telling him about her parents and how mean they were to her, Ric suggested to her that she should move out. Jennifer told him that she couldn't, and that she wanted Ric to kill her parents for her. When Ric realized that she was serious and really wanted to kill them, he stopped talking to her.

After the police received the cell tower records on the phones that had called and texted Jennifer on the night of the murder, they were able to determine the route of one of the phones used. Once they mapped out how the person that was using the phone went that night, they started looking for cameras that might have caught something in the area.

Police spotted an Acura passing slowly by the Hann residence at about 10:00 p.m., then they could see a light in the house go on and then off at 10:02 p.m. It was then that a third call from this number came into Jennifer's phone, and it pinged on the cell tower closest to the Pan home.

On March 19, 2014, the trial began in Newmarket, Ontario. The Crown estimated that it would be a six-month trial, but it ended up being 10 months. There were more than 50 witnesses that testified and over 200 exhibits presented.

Jennifer herself decided to take the stand and testified for seven days, where she spent the time trying to convince the jury that she had originally ordered a hit on her father but had changed her mind about three months later.

The Crown started the case with its opening statement which consisted of Jennifer's 911 call which affected the people in the courtroom dramatically enough to cause people to cry. Jennifer Halajian, the Crown attorney, would start her opening statement, "On Monday, November 8, 2010, just after ten o'clock at night, three men entered the Pan home in Unionville, a quiet neighborhood in Markham. They were in the house for less than twenty minutes. Bich and Hann Pan were left for dead. Bich Pan died. Hann Pan miraculously did not. I am going to talk to you this morning about our theory of what happened that night, and why. Yes, this case is about murder, the planned and deliberate murder of an innocent middle-aged woman and the attempted murder of her husband in their own home on a quiet Monday night in a quiet neighborhood. Murder that was arranged and paid for by their daughter, Jennifer Pan, that woman there." She then pointed her finger at Jennifer and continued, "The woman you heard on the 911 call."

Jennifer was sitting up facing the front of the courtroom, dressed in black turtleneck, black pants and black shoes, which she would wear quite a few of the days in court, as she didn't have any access to her clothes and her family was not helping her out in any way.

"But this case is also about love, love that a girl has for a boy, an obsessive, relentless love, and what she will do to keep him. Love that a father has for his daughter, and what he will do to protect her. Love that a mother has for her child, and what she will do to keep her safe. Love that led to what happened in the basement of an ordinary middle-class house."

To understand what happened on November 8, 2010, you must understand the history, what happened before that, the chronology of what led to that night. Think of it like a map. Jennifer Pan's father, Hann Pan, will testify using a Vietnamese interpreter. He'll describe for you what he knew about their relationship and how he discovered it. He will tell you about the ultimatum he gave to Jennifer Pan to either choose the family or Daniel Wong, and why he gave it. You'll hear what steps he took to keep his daughter from Daniel Wong to protect her, imposing a strict curfew, wanting to know where she was if she left the house. He'll tell you why he was so opposed to the relationship, and he will tell you that in the spring of 2010, Jennifer Pan's lies started to unravel, lies that Hann Pan blamed on Daniel Wong. And so, Hann Pan told his daughter that she will never be with Daniel Wong so long as he and his wife were alive. Jennifer Pan told police that this made her feel trapped. She deeply, bitterly resented it. It made her feel like a part of herself was dead."

The case being presented by Halajian was straight-forward and direct; it would be a story of resentment, love, betrayal, and money. The Crown began to tell the details of Jennifer's lies and made it clear that she was the brains behind the home invasion, with the help of her boyfriend Daniel who brought in the other men to help achieve her goals.

Five people now stood trial for the first-degree murder of Bich Pan and the attempted murder of Hann

Pan, without any forensic evidence. There had been no DNA found at the house, there were no weapons recovered and there were no witnesses to testify about seeing the crime. Of the five people on trial, the Crown also did not know who shot the Pans in their house.

Halajian finished her opening statement by telling the jury, "I told you that three men entered the Pan home that night, but for the rest of this trial, we will focus on these five only, and we will prove that each one of these people, Jennifer, Daniel, Lenford, Eric, and David knowingly participated. That doesn't mean they all pulled the trigger. They didn't, but everyone here had a role. All of them took part in the planning. All of them participated. At least two of them, Jennifer and David, were in the house when Bich and Hann Pan were shot. We know Daniel and Lenford were not there that night, but that doesn't matter, as they were instrumental in putting the plan into motion, and they helped Jennifer carry it out, knowing full well what they were doing."

HUEI HANN PAN TAKES THE STAND

There would be two testimonies that would stand out in the trial; one was Jennifer, and the other would be her father, Hann Pan. When the time came to call Hann to the stand, the courtroom became silent as Hann had not made any statements to the media and had been hidden away in a safe spot by the police.

Hann nervously approached the stand with the help of a victim services member. Hann tried not to focus on the room which was full of reporters and other people that he didn't know. When he first sat, he considered Jennifer's eyes, but only for a moment before he turned away.

JENNIFER PAN TAKES THE STAND

Jennifer took the stand on August 19, 2014, to give her testimony, which would end up taking seven days to complete. It took the first two days alone for Jennifer to tell the jury about all the lies that she had told her parents over the years. The version that she told the court was much the same as what she had confessed to in her interview with Detective Goetz, except for a few major changes.

First, instead of Ric giving her 'Homeboy's' number, she now told the court that she got his number herself and not from Ric. Second, that up until the moment that the intruders broke into the Pan home, she tried to call the attack off. Third, Jennifer admitted to planning to kill her father, but that plan she gave up on when Ric cancelled the deal. Jennifer didn't tell the police of her deal with Ric as she was scared that the police would suspect her in her mother's murder.

Jennifer said that she didn't want to be alive anymore and attempted suicide, but it wouldn't work. She also had a life insurance policy where Felix, her brother, would be the beneficiary, but it wouldn't pay out for suicide. Jennifer then figured the best way around this was to hire someone else to take her life.

Jennifer next told the court that it was only after her boyfriend, Daniel, gave her an iPhone to use so that the two of them could talk, that she noticed some messages from Homeboy. She quickly realized that

Homeboy was dealing drugs for Daniel and thought Homeboy would know how to find someone on the street that could help her commit suicide.

When she approached Homeboy about what it would cost to hire a hitman, he told her it would be somewhere between $10,000 and $15,000. The two then came to an agreement for $10,000. Homeboy would have her murdered within a couple of months.

In the following months, Jennifer said that her relationship with her father began to improve and that he was starting to talk with her again. She said it was at this point she decided that she no longer wanted to die. But when she told this to Homeboy, he refused to let her out of the deal unless she paid him an $8,500. cancellation fee. She agreed to pay him.

It was taking too long for her to come up with the money to pay Homeboy, so on Halloween, he threatened to shoot her while she was handing out candy to the trick-or-treaters. Scared, Jennifer told Homeboy that she would meet him and give him some of the money.

Jennifer claims the next time she heard from Homeboy was on the morning of November 8, when he texted her the *"To after work OK will be game time."* She said that this text was not about a plot to kill her parents, it was about paying him the money she owed him. She said that after talking with Homeboy, she tried to gather up the whole cancellation fee.

Jennifer then admits that she unlocked her front door after receiving another text, this time saying,

"VIP entry." When the question came up of what happened to her iPhone's SIM card, she responded by saying that the intruder stole her SIM card out of her phone.

Jennifer then began to cry in court when she explained that she didn't want anything to happen to her parents and felt helpless when the intruders took them downstairs. She said that she even screamed out for her mother, who in turn was screaming that she wanted her daughter with her.

The cross-examination of Jennifer was primarily centered on the fact that she had plenty of opportunity to go to the police and notify them before the home invasion happened, but she didn't. She also had plenty of chances to tell them the truth after the murder, but she didn't. Were the jury supposed to believe that those were the actions of a loving daughter?

The prosecutor then challenged Jennifer's story about finding Homeboy's messages from the iPhone that her boyfriend Daniel Wong gave to her only to keep him out of the police investigation. This was also only after she first named her friend's roommate Ric and that lie fell through.

The prosecution then aggressively stated, "Your mother is brutally murdered in your basement twenty meters below you, and what you do is go into the police station twice in the following week and lie to them. And there's only one reason you lie to the police the day after your mother is shot in the head, to keep Jennifer Pan from getting in trouble." Jennifer quickly responded, "I was scared."

"Right, because it's more important to you in your world that you stay out of trouble than the police find your mother's killers, that's your thought process, Jennifer Pan is about Jennifer Pan." Jennifer snapped back, "Disagree."

"Then why don't you sacrifice yourself as the good daughter so that they can find the real killers of your mother?" the prosecutor asked.

"That's why I'm here."

"Why weren't you there in November 2010?" he replied.

"Because I was very scared."

"You're not scared. You're selfish and you're greedy."

It only took the jury four days after the 10-month trial ended to decide on Jennifer and four of her cohorts' fate. The fifth member that was on trial, Eric Carty, was severed from the trial, as his lawyer became ill and the case was too complicated and had gone on too long for Eric to retain a new attorney, so he would be tried later.

The four defendants were called back into court for the decision on December 13, 2014, and Jennifer appeared to be happy and was smiling like she was about to get an award. The other three defendants appeared with no emotion on their face and didn't make eye contact with any of the jury.

The foreman stood and looked at each of the accused and one by one read out the guilty verdicts.

The only person to change their demeanor was Jennifer, as she lowered her face towards the floor when they pronounced her guilty. There were some screams in the courtroom and Daniel Wong's mother ran out.

HAAN IMPACT STATEMENT

"When I lost my wife, I lost my daughter at the same time, I don't feel like I have a family anymore. Some say I should feel lucky to be alive, but I feel like I am dead too. I hope that my daughter Jennifer thinks about what has happened to her family and can become a good honest person someday."

Hann is unable to work because of the injuries he suffered on the night of the home invasion. He also has bad anxiety and can't sleep at night without having nightmares. He doesn't want to live in his house anymore but has been unable to sell it as nobody seems to want to buy it. He now lives away from the house with his brother.

SENTENCING

The sentencing occurred on January 23, 2015; Jennifer was given the maximum penalty of two life sentences for the first-degree murder of her mother and the attempted murder of her father with no chance of parole for at least twenty-five years. She will be in prison until at least 2036. Daniel Wong, David Mylvaganam, and Lenford Crawford each were sentenced the same as Jennifer.

Eric Carty bargained with the Crown to take an 18-year sentence in return for his admissions. He was already serving 25 years for the murder of somebody else that was not related to the Pan home invasion.

Eric Carty later filed an appeal of his conviction arguing that the 911 call should not have been allowed in trial. He further found fault with the trial judge's failure to give a no probative value order to Carty's past indecent behavior, namely that he fled and was on the lam for more than a year.

In October of 2017, the court rejected both arguments, but noted that the trial judge did err in allowing the 911 call as hearsay evidence rather than as a spontaneous statement.

In 2015, Jennifer Pan filed for an appeal to her convictions arguing that the jury selection was fundamentally flawed, resulting in a jury that was not properly composed.

Crimes Canada Collection

**(Click on Image will take you to Amazon US
These books are available WORLDWIDE on Amazon)**

THE KILLER HANDYMAN
WILLIAM PATRICK FYFE

C.L. SWINNEY

CRIMES CANADA
TRUE CRIMES THAT SHOCKED THE NATION VOL. 7

Hell's Angels
BIKER WARS
the Rock Machine Massacres

RJ PARKER

CRIMES CANADA
TRUE CRIMES THAT SHOCKED THE NATION VOL. 8

THE DARK STRANGLER
EARLE LEONARD NELSON

MICHAEL NEWTON

CRIMES CANADA
TRUE CRIMES THAT SHOCKED THE NATION VOL. 9

ALCOHOL MURDERS
TRUE STORY OF SERIAL KILLER
GILBERT PAUL JORDAN

HARRIET FOX

CRIMES CANADA
TRUE CRIMES THAT SHOCKED THE NATION VOL. 10

PETER WOODCOCK
CANADA'S YOUNGEST SERIAL KILLER

MARK BOURRIE

CRIMES CANADA
TRUE CRIMES THAT SHOCKED THE NATION VOL. 11

CLIFFORD OLSON

THE BEAST OF BRITISH COLUMBIA

ELIZABETH BRODERICK

CRIMES CANADA
TRUE CRIMES THAT SHOCKED THE NATION VOL. 12

TAKING TORI

THE TRUE STORY OF
TERRI-LYNNE McCLINTIC &
MICHAEL RAFFERTY

KELLY BANASKI

CRIMES CANADA
TRUE CRIMES THAT SHOCKED THE NATION VOL. 13

BANDITS & RENEGADES
HISTORICAL TRUE CRIME STORIES

SPECIAL EDITION

EDWARD BUTTS

CRIMES CANADA
TRUE CRIMES THAT SHOCKED THE NATION VOL. 14

INVISIBLE VICTIMS
MISSING AND MURDERED INDIGENOUS WOMEN

KATHERINE McCARTHY

CRIMES CANADA
TRUE CRIMES THAT SHOCKED THE NATION VOL. 15

ABOUT THE AUTHOR

Alan R Warren is one of the current hosts of the House of Mystery Radio Show that is heard on KKNW 1150 AM in Seattle and is syndicated in Utah on KVFX 98.3 FM and KYAH 540 AM in Salt Lake City and KFNX 1100 AM Phoenix. He has written three best selling True Crime books and articles for True Crime Case Files Magazine and Serial Killer Magazine.

Alan achieved his Masters in Music at the University of Washington and his minor in Criminology. He also has his recording and sound engineering certificate from the Award-Winning Bullfrog Studios in Vancouver B.C., Canada.

Follow on *Amazon*

Crimes Canada: True Crimes that Shocked the Nation (Book 19)

Complete Series LINK

CHECK OUT SOME OF ALAN'S OTHER BOOKS

Above Suspicion: The True Story of Serial Killer Russell Williams

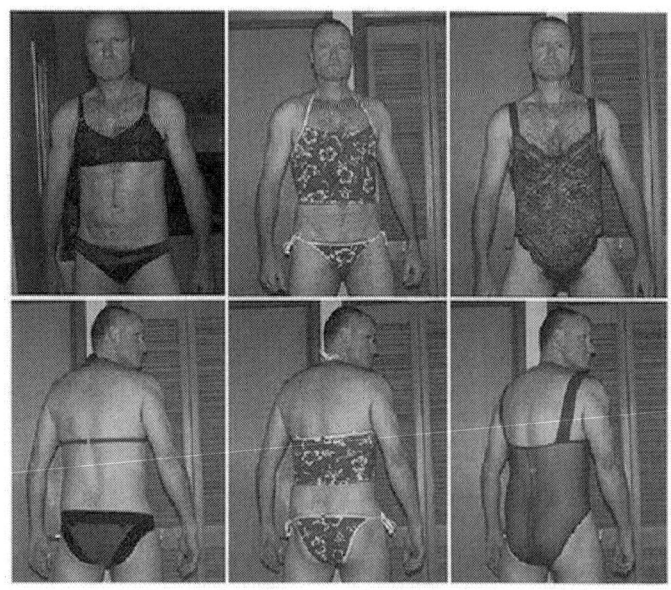

This is the true story of Russell Williams; once the model of a military man, he now sits convicted of a series of crimes that include two counts of first-degree murder, brutal sexual assaults, and 82 home invasions that included a series of strange thefts.

Colonel Russell Williams once seemed the embodiment of the military ideals of duty and honor, a pilot for the Prime Minister and Queen Elizabeth of England, commander of the secret Canadian Air Force base in the Persian Gulf, and in 2009 appointed commanding officer of Canada's largest, most important Air Force base in Trenton, Ontario.

Russell Williams's fall from grace is a frightening reminder of the unpredictability of human behavior.

CHAPTER ONE 1

MURDER OF CORPORAL COMEAU

Corporal Marie-France Comeau was born into a military family in 1972; her dad was a Canadian Armed Forces medic and one of her grandfathers had earned honours as a pilot in World War II. Growing up listening to the war stories of both men greatly excited the young girl, who at an early age made an important decision; she would join the Air Force, and ended up among the crew that escorted Prime Minister Stephen Harper to Mumbai in November 2009.

Now back from that trip that she had always dreamed about, she was looking forward to telling her boyfriend all about it. However, while she was away, a predator had been on his own trip, only to her home. One week before, knowing that she was away, Williams had made a reconnaissance trip to her home.

He found the rear basement window unlocked. It was large enough for him to fit through, where he checked out her bathroom and closets to make sure that there were no signs of a man living there. He also couldn't resist the bedroom, where he would find her sex toys, bras and panties, some of which he couldn't help but to try on, and even take with him to his own home.

It was 11 P.M., and while on the phone with her boyfriend, setting up dinner plans with him so that she could share all the events of her recent trip, Williams had made the same trip to her house. He was now in her basement, waiting for her to go to bed and fall asleep.

After finishing her call, Marie-France realized she had not seen her cat, Bixby. Starting her search, she headed for the basement, knowing that was his favorite hiding spot. " Bixby, where are you?" she yelled from the top of the stairs. She turned on the basement lights and started down the stairs to find her cat." There you are." She walked toward the cat, bent down to pick him up, just then, she saw a dark figure behind the furnace, and screamed loudly.

Knowing he must silence her right away, he smashed his flashlight over her head. This only made her want to fight, even though she could feel the blood on her head. It took several more blows before she would fall backwards.

Williams then lunged on top of her, which smeared her blood across the cement floor. He bound her wrists with rope. He stood her up and pushed her against a metal jack support post, where a steel pin ripped into her upper back. He then tied her firmly to the post and covered her mouth with duct tape.

Now that his victim was secured, he would now make sure that they would not be interrupted. He took her house key, which had been left on the kitchen table, and snapped it off in the lock of the front door, so that nobody that had a key could get in. He then headed for her bedroom, ripped the comforter off her bed and covered her bedroom window with it.

He then headed back to the basement, not paying attention to the trail of blood that he was leaving with his shoes. He removed the duct tape from her mouth and cut the ties to the post so that he could bring her upstairs to the bedroom. While starting up the stairs, Marie started to scream. He quickly grabbed her head and smashed it against the wall, creating a spray of blood and a head-shaped crater. Marie now dropped to the floor unconscious.

Williams now felt compelled to get his camera and take four pictures of her lying naked and bleeding on the floor, including a close-up on her vagina and the cuts on her breasts and face.

Williams then carried her up to her bedroom and placed her onto the bed, placing her in a fetal position. He grabbed a towel from the bathroom and wrapped it around her head, covering her eyes and nose, then wrapping it with duct tape to keep it in place. He then set up his camcorder on a tripod at the foot of the bed, focusing on the still unconscious Marie, pressed record, and started to undress.

He climbed onto the bed wearing nothing except on his face, which was covered with a black skull cap. He forced Marie onto her back and spread her legs and lined her up for penetration. She then moaned "no" as he began to rape her. As not to care about her protest, he grabbed his camera, which he had placed on the bed, and started taking pictures of the penetration.

After 17 minutes of raping her in several different positions, only stopping to take random pictures, Williams then removed his face mask and smiled smugly at the camcorder while rubbing her breasts and stomach. All the while, Marie was telling him to "get out, get out" and "I want you to leave," but he didn't answer.

Williams then whispered, "Stay there," and again got up from the bed, smiled into the camcorder again, and grabbed and squeezed some KY jelly onto his fingers. He moved back towards the bed, and applied the lubricant to her genitals, and climbed back on top of her. After a few more minutes of intercourse, he looked back into the camera, withdrew and carefully caught his ejaculate into his cupped hand. Now on his way into the bathroom, she wondered if she could try and escape?

Hearing the toilet flush, she slid herself off the bed. She heard Williams walk into the living room, so she headed for the bathroom, and slammed the door closed behind her, hoping to get the door locked behind her before he noticed she was no longer on the bed.

But she wasn't fast enough. He smashed through the door and threw her against the bathroom wall. He grabbed her by the hair and dragged her back into the bedroom, pushing her into a seated position on the bed. "Now stay here," he told her boldly. He forced intercourse on her again, followed by another round of photographs.

After he finished, Williams then rifled through her drawers, taking out select pieces of underwear and laying them onto her body, and took more pictures. It was like he wanted to model her in different garments, and create a catalogue for himself.

He then started placing them into his duffel bag, perhaps as future souvenirs that he could have for future benefit to relieve himself with. She then began to moan loudly, "Oh Oh Oh" and move back and forth on the bed. He quickly lay down beside her, and said "Shh shh." "No no please," she replied, "I don't want to die." "You're not going to die," Williams answered quickly. The struggle went on like this back and forth for several minutes.

He placed more duct tape around her face, covering her mouth and nose this time, according to the police transcripts. she then died of suffocation, the result of her airways being covered with duct tape.

It was now 4 a.m. and he had to beat an important meeting in Ottawa, about a three-hour drive, so Williams had no time to go home. Before leaving, he threw all the sheets from her bed and the comforter that he had hung over the window into the wash and doused them in bleach, not realizing that he had left his shoe print in the trail of blood, a mistake that would soon catch up to him.

The next morning, November 25, Comeau's boyfriend became worried as she had not shown up for work, and he had just spoken to her the previous night, very unlike Marie-France.

He then went over to her home and let himself in. Outside, Comeau's neighbour, Terry Alexander, was welcoming a plumber who had come to his house for repairs.

He recalls France's boyfriend suddenly bursting out of the home running across the street, tears running down his face. "Did you see any strange people or cars around here?" he shouted. "She's lying dead inside," he said before breaking down into sobs.

Investigations concluded two days later that Comeau's death had been a homicide. Investigators from Northumberland OPP (Ontario Provincial Police) spent a few weeks looking for evidence, even stripping the floors down to the concrete and ripping out the cabinets in the kitchen.

The neighbours in the small town were afraid, and rumours began to spread, many having different theories on the events that had taken place. Many neighbours had not known her well. Terry

Alexander spoke of her shyness, and another neighbour said that he had never seen her around the block. Her ex-boyfriend, Alain Plante, who was a basic training instructor, had spent more than four years with her, and his son Etienne had loved the woman like his mother.

The Corporal was buried on December 4, 2009, at the National Military Cemetery in Ottawa. Many family members, fellow military officers, and friends attended the ceremony. An ironic and perhaps angering fact is that, as her commanding officer, Williams was tasked with writing an official letter of condolence to her father. He also attended the funeral and participated, reading a eulogy for Comeau, who until now, nobody could have imagined had been murdered by the Colonel himself.

On Amazon

Kindle - http://amzn.to/2EQteLm

Paperback - http://amzn.to/2qeNdA6

Audiobook - http://amzn.to/2lNFwvk

Blood Thirst: True Story of Rapist, Vampire, and Serial Killer, Wayne Boden

Known as the "Vampire Rapist" or "Strangler Bill" for his distinctive modus operandi, Wayne Boden would rape, strangle, and bite the breasts of his victims.

His murdering rampage would continue in two cities over three years; he was only caught by superior evidence gathering and the help of an orthodontist. This book asks the question "How do we really know our boyfriend or lover when we don't want to ask the questions, not only because we don't want to know the answers for what they will tell us about them, but because of what they tell us about ourselves?"

True crime author Alan R. Warren takes you through the details of the case, including dental impressions used in court to convict Boden, a first in Canadian history, as well as Boden's escape from a maximum-security prison.

CHAPTER ONE

HUMBLE BEGINNINGS OF WAYNE BODEN

'We come to Beginnings only at the End' – **William Throsby Bridges**

Wayne Clifford Boden was born on January 1, 1948. He grew up in the quiet tree-lined streets of Dundas, Ontario. Located only 13 miles west of Hamilton, Ontario, in the picturesque Dundas Valley, it was a town with historic 19th century buildings and a population of about 12,000 people in the 1960s. It was known as being the home to the famous comedian of SCTV Dave Thomas and Major League Baseball pitcher Pete Ward.

Wayne's father, Albert, died in 1966 when Wayne was 18 years old. He wasn't close with his father, who was very strict and not known as very affectionate. He had worked in a factory for 30 years. Wayne's mother, Laverna, would have been 34 when she gave birth to him. She was the consummate housewife and believed her goal in life was to keep a well-run home clean and always have the dinner on the table at the same time every night.

Laverna was not close to her son at all. She was more of a school headmistress than mother to Wayne, only communicating with nothing but duties for him to perform. Laverna was never known to give a kind word to anybody, and she constantly complained about how people around never knew how to do their jobs correctly. An example would be how she would always tell the milkman how he had got their order wrong, delivered too warm of milk, and was always late for his delivery.

Wayne was not close to his mother and didn't really like her. She was not an educated woman and couldn't read or write at all. He found himself always having to help her with these things in her duties as a housewife, such as writing up the order for the milkman. Sometimes he would find himself so frustrated with her. He thought that she was stupid and was embarrassed by this.

He found himself telling the teachers at school that his mother was not alive because he didn't want to tell them about her. Why couldn't his mother be like his teachers? Not only were they women, but they were smart and could read and write.

Wayne's parents had never shown any signs of affection in front of him. He was never allowed into their bedroom; it was one of many rooms that was simply out of bounds for him to be in. The main living room and kitchen were also off limits to him. It was a very isolating experience for Wayne.

It was an accident the first time that he had caught a glimpse into his parents' room. He was outside of their doorway when his mother came out with a large load of sheets in her arms and she was unable to close the door right away. He noticed that there were two beds in the room. This was not an uncommon practice in the 1950s and '60s. Quite often the master room would be furnished with two twin beds, not the standard double or queen size beds of today. Even on the popular television shows or movies of the time, the main characters always had twin beds portrayed in their bedrooms.

This one quick glimpse led Wayne to fantasize on how it must have been to be married. He developed the idea that you only would sleep with your wife when you were trying to have children and that the wife's duty was simply to run the household, almost more of a job and not a loving relationship. This was probably where he started to put the placing of a woman as second to the man in the house.

Wayne did not have any brothers or sisters either. He would come home right after school, as his mother would be watching to see what time he would arrive. If he was late even by five minutes, she would scold him for taking his time when he had work to complete.

After his list of chores were completed, he would show up for his dinner which was exactly at five thirty, and she would first check to see that his hands had been washed before he could even sit at the table. Dinner would then be served, and the three of them would sit and eat in silence, with the only noise being the sound of their grandfather clock ticking in the dining room that Wayne had never been allowed in. He knew the clock by sound far better than he ever would have by sight.

After he would finish dinner and be excused from the table, he would go straight into his room and close his door. He would not see his parents again until morning. His mother would walk down the hall and stop at his door at 8 p.m. every night and listen. He would just lie there silent, even holding his breath, careful not to make any noise, or she would yell at him that it was time to be asleep. After she walked away and went into her own bedroom, he would resume about his activities.

Wayne always spent his nights alone in his room, never inviting anyone over. He didn't want to have to deal with bringing somebody into his home and having them face his mother. Not only that, he never had any close friends in his school days, so there was nobody to invite.

He would just lie on his bed listening to CKOC AM 1150 out of Hamilton on his transistor radio alone. He liked hearing the latest in music, and he would close his eyes and dream that it was him singing the song. He had this fantasy that he was going to become a popular pop artist and all the pretty girls would stand in large lines to wait to hear him sing. Now there is no record of him ever trying to learn to sing, or him being part of the music or theatre department at school. Instead, he ended up joining the football team at school.

Boden went to Glendale secondary school until the mid-1960s. He was thought of as quiet, muscular, and played on the school senior football team. He was well liked by his teachers, as he was respectful and quiet. Wayne seemed to admire his teachers and always went out of his way to help them as much as he could. He would clean their chalk boards, carry books, and quite often stay behind to help in any way that he could. This affection towards teachers took a twist in the very near future, not anything that people would expect.

Wayne's nice helpful behavior towards his teachers was not something a lot of other students in the school appreciated. Though he was liked by most other students, the most misbehaved students thought of Wayne a 'suck' or 'teacher's pet' and would always call him names. Wayne being a football player, with the tough reputation that came with that, almost forced him to stand up for himself against such ridicule. He would find himself getting into several fights at school, one of them quite bloody with fellow student George Tirone where Boden was the winner.

Wayne tried his luck at being a model. He was handsome, well-built and clean cut. Most of the girls in school would also comment how handsome he was. But Wayne was extremely shy, would never look at people in the eyes. He would also not talk much; many times at parties, he would sit by himself in the corner of the room and could go unnoticed for hours. Wayne never had any girlfriends during his high school days. It is more likely that he wasn't secure enough to ask any girl to go out with him.

This kind of attitude was not very conducive with being a model. He was also extremely shy about taking off his clothes. Though he was nicely built, he felt the need to keep himself covered completely and wouldn't even shower with the other boys after playing football. Consider that being a model would mean he would have to be more aggressive and face the camera and certainly not be afraid of taking off his shirt, or more. Additionally, there were just no modeling jobs in this small town.

He then tried different sales positions around town, but again, being such a small town, there just wasn't much opportunity. Wayne found it real hard to make any sales when his customer base was so small. He felt he would have to move to a larger city, but he didn't know where. At first, he tried Hamilton, which was a short distance from home and certainly a much bigger center to work in. But Wayne grew tired of Hamilton rather quickly. Hamilton, though it was larger, didn't have the culture base that he was looking for. Hamilton was known as a steel town. It was Canada's version of Pittsburgh, where the base of the economy was steel manufacturing. With that came a lot of steel workers and their families that were not looking for nightlife, parties and male models.

Wayne had not adjusted very well. He was extremely awkward around others and couldn't hold a conversation for any length of time. His father died when he was young, and his mother was quite a bit older. Not having any brothers or sisters, he spent most of his time alone, with no social interaction.

It was sometime in 1967 when Wayne moved to Montreal to 1849 Dorch #24 and worked as a travelling salesman. He maintained his well-built frame from his high school football days, with the current trend of bushy sideburns. He was considered to be mild mannered and very polite, the kind of man that you could take home to your parents. Moving to the big city also gave him lots of young people to meet and clubs to socialize in.

On Amazon

Kindle - http://amzn.to/2CNYolP

Paperback - http://amzn.to/2ET5SF6

REFERENCES

Crime Watch Daily (15 February 2017) Did 'Tiger Parenting' prompt daughter toward suicide, or murder?

Lau, Joyce (8 November 2016). "A murder in Toronto and the dark side of the Asian immigrant dream" South China Morning Post

Ho, Karen K. (22 July 2015). "Jennifer Pan's Revenge: The inside story of a golden child, the killers she hired, and the parents she wanted dead" Toronto Life

Wang, Yanan (27 July 2015). "Tragedy of 'golden' daughter's fall resonates with Asian immigrant children" Washington Post

Paola Loriggio, The Canadian Press (24 January 2015). "Jennifer Pan, Toronto woman whose plot to kill parents left mother dead, gets life in prison" National Post

"Jennifer Pan sentenced to life without parole for 25 years" cbc.ca. 23 January 2015.

"Jennifer Pan: Life with no parole for 25 years in murder of mother, attempted murder of father" thestar.com. 23 January 2015

Brown, Vanessa (11 December 2016) "When Chinese cubs turn on their Tiger Parents" News.com.au

Grimaldi, Jeremy (13 November 2016) "The story behind the confession of Jennifer Pan" The Star.com

Regina Vs. Pan et al. Trial transcripts

Made in the USA
Lexington, KY
27 January 2018